THE PATHWAY OF HOLINESS

A GUIDE FOR SINNERS

JOHN WHITE

InterVarsity Press
Downers Grove, Illinois

InterVarsity Press® is the book-publishing division of InterVarsity Christian Fellowship®, a student movement active on campus at hundreds of universities, colleges and schools of nursing in the United States of America, and a member movement of the International Fellowship of Evangelical Students. For information about local and regional activities, write Public Relations Dept., InterVarsity Christian Fellowship, 6400 Schroeder Rd., P.O. Box 7895, Madison, WI 53707-7895.

All Scripture quotations, unless otherwise indicated, are taken from the HOLY BIBLE, NEW INTERNATIONAL VERSION®. NIV®. Copyright ©1973, 1978, 1984 by International Bible Society. Used by permission of Zondervan Publishing House. All rights reserved.

Cover photograph: Dennis Frates

ISBN 0-8308-1980-0

Printed in the United States of America ♾

Library of Congress Cataloging-in-Publication Data

White, John, 1924 Mar. 5-
    The pathway of holiness: a guide for sinners/John White.
        p.   cm.
    Includes bibliographical references.
    ISBN 0-8303-1980-0 (pbk.: alk. paper)
    1. Holiness.   I. Title.
BT767.W47   1996
234'.8—dc20   95-50980
                                                                                      CIP

| 20 | 19 | 18 | 17 | 16 | 15 | 14 | 13 | 12 | 11 | 10 | 9 | 8 | 7 | 6 | 5 | 4 | 3 | 2 | 1 |
| 12 | 11 | 10 | 09 | 08 | 07 | 06 | 05 | 04 | 03 | 02 | 01 | 00 | 99 | 98 | 97 | 96 |

PART 1

THE
DESCENT
INTO
HOLINESS

---

*D*ESCENT? ISN'T THAT THE WRONG WORD? HOW CAN YOU *DESCEND* INTO holiness?

This first section of this book deals with getting off our high horses. Chapter one considers what holiness is and looks at the problems of the love of a holy God. Chapter two discusses ways in which your own Bible reading can become a key to holiness. We get off our high horse when we realize that the Bible was not given to us so that we could master it, but because the God of Scripture wants to master us as we read it. We are not to master the Bible but to be mastered by it. And again, because few of us like to admit, even to ourselves, that we are absolutely helpless to overcome sins we have fought for years, and because that unwillingness arises from pride, I devote chapter three to the dangers of pride. We need to look at pride, the first sin, very carefully. Repenting of pride is getting off our high horse.

Chapters four and five have to do with repentance, false and true. In a book I once wrote about repentance,[1] I compared it with an earthquake, a profound shaking coinciding with a new awakening to a reality we had forgotten. God's dealings over the years build to a climax—then *bang!* the earthquake hits. From that point on we find ourselves living in an earthquake zone. Repentance opens the doorway to a life of repentance.

Chapter six talks about worship. You ask, isn't worship a rather advanced aspect of Christian faith? Indeed no. Highbrow perhaps, but not advanced, since a highbrow approach is half the trouble. We were made to worship. We were saved in order that we might worship, and to worship one God alone—not Mammon the god of money, nor Baal, one of the gods of sex, nor any other god but God. He saved you because he wanted to be worshiped. Worship and adoration come at the *beginning* of the Christian life. It is part of the descent into sanctity. You get off your high horse when you realize the need to fall on your face before God.

Chapter seven deals with a more contemporary problem. Just now many churches in Britain—in fact all over the world—are experiencing services in which people behave strangely,[2] services that may continue half the night. During times of refreshing and renewal this sort of thing sometimes happens, and there has long been confusion about whether these experiences are experiences of empowering or of sanctification. Some Christians feel that this is the way to become holy. What is evident is that the meetings can be an occasion of getting off our high horses again, as we face the relinquishment of cherished understandings, admitting that we may not know all we think. Chapter seven discusses the issues raised by such phenomena.

Finally, chapter eight begins the ascent. Many of us have been discouraged by an unending struggle with secret sins. We are ashamed of them, ashamed of what we are, and have been disappointed repeatedly. A great weariness has come upon us. And I must not deceive you. The struggle in this life will be unending. Yet God wishes to lift us up. The struggle is not futile, for steady progress can be made.

Specific forms of sin can be plucked up by the roots. But God must decide which one has to come up first. What chapter eight talks about is what God has already done in you—the righteousness you already have. Often I have found that this is the real key to making progress.

It is crucial that our feet be set on the pathway to holiness. Therefore this book is not concerned primarily with what holiness is but with how you get to be holy. Both as individuals and as the church we must pursue that goal relentlessly. I believe God has given us a Word that can be understood by anybody—at least by anyone whose heart seeks God. That is "where the rubber meets the road." Seeking God simply *has* to be what you are after. I believe that "the wayfaring man, though a fool" need not err when reading Scripture. We can grow into God's holiness.

1

THE
NEED FOR
HOLINESS

---

*T*ODAY ANYTHING GOES, AND IT ALL SEEMS TO BE GOING DOWNHILL. NEW laws multiply to control the downward rush, only to increase its speed. Among the philosophies those laws embody, moral relativism bids to be the doctrine of the day. People used to say you could do anything you liked provided you didn't hurt anybody. Today lawyers defend people who have damaged others very seriously. We have a justice system in which lawyers get thieves and murderers off on technicalities and child molesters get out of jail for good behavior, while innocent people are wrongly condemned. Public outcries arise over these and many other matters.

The world views the church as no better than themselves. They are almost right. We lust for money, sex and power. Church scandals abound, and we display a surprisingly high sin rate. Christian counselors, to whom many Christians turn for help, tend not to support church discipline. They may support the *idea* of church discipline but find themselves faced with conflicting loyalties because they are required to maintain client confidentiality. Inevitably Christian counselors may be driven to help perpetuate rather than solve the problem of the church's unholy behavior.

So where do we go from here? The world leads the church too often, whereas the church should lead the world. The church can do so, once God's holiness begins to invade us. For God is a God of holiness. A day is coming soon when the world will tremble before the holiness of God as it shines through the church.

The Need for Holiness

What is holiness? Is it the absence of sin in our lives? Is it Christian perfection? Why should we be interested in it?

I can think of a number of reasons we should want to be holy. First, if we are not holy, nobody around us will want to be, either. There is a delicate balance between the individual and the community. Second, until we are holy, we will not "see" God—that is, we will know little of his drawing near us. "Make every effort . . . to be holy; without holiness no one will see the Lord" (Heb 12:14). Seeing him, we become holier; becoming holier, we see him better.

Third, the world, though opposed to the church, spends little time thinking about Christians at all. It is a question of impatient indifference rather than outright hostility. It is not the pastor's responsibility to correct this indifference, but our own. Holiness will begin in our church when *we* start being holy. Holiness is a contagion. Sooner or later it begins to spread outward from anyone who is holy.

Fourth, the world will awaken to *the fear of God* when it sees a holy church. People will begin either to tremble or else to grind their teeth with rage and defiance before the presence of God in the church. The first sign of a spiritual awakening will be when many people run to church to find out about Jesus, while others hate and dread the God of the church. Most revivals have seen waves of anxious inquirers along with increasingly hostile mockers.

Finally, we ought to be holy because the God who loves us wants to impart holiness to us—as a gift. He wants fellowship with us, wants to draw near us. However, he has to be careful, lest he should burn us. God and sin don't get along, and we all have sin in us. So he longs with a tender, unsatisfied longing. He wants to uproot sins in us one by one—even though it will take the rest of our lives—so that he can have intimacy with you and me. Whenever his Holy Spirit convicts us, it is always with our freedom in mind, never our condemnation.

Holiness arises in the person of God. It represents the quintessence of God's character. Holiness is to be and to act like God. When God acts, he acts in holy love. J. I. Packer goes so far as to say, "*God is holy love.*"[1] After all, "God is love" (1 Jn 4:8). He is also supremely holy.

God loves us and wants to know us. His whole desire is toward us. He reaches out in tenderness, knowing all about our struggles and pains. His ways are ways of pleasantness, and all his paths are peace.

At first such statements as I have made would seem to solve problems rather than create them. God is holy love. His very being expresses itself in love toward all people everywhere, and in particular toward his special people, those who claim to follow him, whether Jew or Gentile.

The Danger

Let's go back a bit. As a Christian, you began to be holy when you joined the Christian ranks: "you were washed, you were sanctified, you were justified in the name of the Lord Jesus Christ and by the Spirit of our God" (1 Cor 6:11). When that happened, wealth, money, power, sex became—if only for a few seconds—of no consequence. Lust (the worship of any craving and the consequent bondage to dark powers) died in that moment, but soon revived.

A moment ago I said that we pursue holiness because without it we will not see God. Seeing him, glorious as it is, has its dangers. In a total eclipse of the sun, all you could see is a sort of blackish moon with a circle of light around it, a *corona*. And we are warned that even the corona could cause partial blindness if we looked at it with a naked eye. We are supposed to look through smoked glass or with some other filter.

A children's story I read called *The Voyage of the Dawn Treader*[2] had an earth that was flat. Its eastern edge held a fascination for the voyagers, an assortment of children, adults and talking animals traveling together on a ship. The nearer the *Dawn Treader* got to the eastern edge of the world, the sweeter the seawater became. Soon the travelers were drinking sweet seawater, which made their eyes strong enough to stare directly at the sun.

Seeing God is like that. The more we journey along the pathway of holiness, the more we drink draughts of a life-giving something. Our eyes grow stronger, our vision clearer.

Peril remains, especially at times when God's Spirit is being poured out. Two different men have told me that in God's presence they recently found themselves as D. L. Moody once did: they cried out in terror, "No more!" God's nearness was such that they felt they were in danger of losing their lives. Were they? I doubt it, but I know the feeling. It is the feeling that leading men in Israel once experienced as they witnessed God's presence on Mount Sinai. Moses reminded the people,

> When you heard the voice out of the darkness, while the mountain was ablaze with fire, all the leading men of your tribes and your elders came to me. And you said, "The LORD our God has shown us his glory and his majesty, and we have heard his voice from the fire. Today we have seen that a man can live even if God speaks with him. But now, why should we die? This great fire will consume us, and we will die if we hear the voice of the LORD our God any longer. For what mortal man has ever heard the voice of the living God speaking out of fire, as we have, and survived?" (Deut 5:23-26)

Their fear was real. And from time to time God has to teach us, as he taught them. It is a lesson that must be learned again and again. God's holy presence can kill us. We have to take it in small doses, gradually growing more able to stand in his presence.

Yet once you have been bitten by the bug, awakened to the longing, you can never entirely lose it. It will awaken, however far you wander, to haunt you with longing.

D. L. Moody's "slightly too close encounter" occurred in New York in the summer or fall of 1871. He was on a "begging" (his word) trip to wealthy men in New York, but his heart was not in what he was doing. He describes the encounter himself.

> Well, one day, in the city of New York—oh, what a day!—I cannot describe it, I seldom refer to it; it is almost too sacred an experience to name. . . . I can only say that God revealed himself to me, and I had such an experience of his love that I had to ask him to stay his hand. I went to preaching again. The sermons were not different; I did not present any new truths, and yet hundreds were converted.[3]

This encounter was an impartation of power, and I shall go into details about such encounters in chapter seven.

Divine Jealousy

There is peril in being loved by God, because God's love is holy and *jealous* love. Paul told the Corinthian church, "I am jealous for you with a godly jealousy. I promised you to one husband, to Christ, so that I might present you as a pure virgin to him" (2 Cor 11:2).

Thus it is in the jealousy of love that the problem lies. The same love that can ravish us can also consume by its flames. And though the idea of being ravished in the flames of holy love may sound poetic, even romantic, we are not sure whether we want such a dangerous kind of love. Nevertheless, this is how it is. The flames of divine love can kill our physical bodies. They have done so in the past and will do so in the future. For the same love that will ravish some will be deadly danger to others, especially in those periods when God's Spirit is poured out.

Love is not real love unless it includes jealousy. How can that be? To us jealousy is mean and petty. Clearly God cannot be mean and petty. No, the beauty of God's holy character is not marred by his jealousy, which is but a burning desire that we become like him as his children. But we must face it.

So what is divine jealousy? When we speak of being jealous, we often mean that we are *envious* of someone. That person may have something we want—brains, beauty, wealth, privilege or whatever. God is certainly not jealous in that sense. He needs nothing, for he has all he could ever want.

A man or woman whose spouse is unfaithful can have a jealousy that includes many strong emotions—rage, bitterness, love, fear, hatred and envy, to name only a few. But God knows no bitterness, fear or envy. Predominant in his attitude toward any Christian, as well as toward the corporate body of believers, is love. God's rage and hatred are an integral part of his love. They arise out of his love.

God's love is directed to the unfaithful lover still. His rage is over two things: the sin of infidelity and the fact that we are being cheated. His rage burns against the powers of darkness—not because God is afraid of them or fears that they have more power than he or are more "attractive." Rather, he knows we have been fooled. We have sold our birthright for a "mess of pottage." Thus his anger burns against us and against the cruelty and viciousness of dark powers that have deceived us.

But because God's love also includes patience and kindness, he is slow to bring discipline to bear on us. This is how he revealed himself to Moses: "And he passed in front of Moses, proclaiming, 'The LORD, the LORD, the compassionate and gracious God, slow to anger, abounding in love and faithfulness, maintaining love to thousands, and forgiving wickedness, rebellion and sin' " (Ex 34:6-7).

He is forgiving. And as we learn in Exodus 20, he is jealous of our worship of any god, whether Mammon or Baal or any of the fallen angelic beings that try to play god. Most of us worship one or another of them, and some of us worship both Mammon and Baal—and others as well. We do so without knowing what we are doing. He knows the danger that this represents, and the cruelty we will suffer in consequence. For though the old gods may treat us well when it suits their purposes, they will toss us aside as refuse when they have finished with us.

God's love calls all men and women into a relationship that God compares with marriage. He wants to *know* us in the old-fashioned and sexual sense of the term. God's design for marriage is one husband, one wife, *only*. He has the same design for the marriage of his Son. *The man or the woman who does not experience jealous anger, even jealous rage, over a partner's infidelity has a love that is not worth calling love at all.* Such "love" is pitifully inadequate. The true jealous love will protect the life of a false lover, as Hosea protected his false wife in his home, maintaining his protective care while not enforcing intimacy. In this way Hosea modeled the patient and compassionate love of God to Israel. God protects our lives even though he may have to remove us from this world to do so. He does not cease to love us. It is because of his love that he first sought us.

Given our faithlessness, God's rage had to be placated. It had to be plunged as a sword into the heart of Messiah, Son of God. The scene, humanly speaking, arose through history's most horrendous blunder. At the same time it was the greatest manifestation of divine love and, paradoxically, history's most significant turning point.

Jehovah lifted up His rod:
O Christ it fell on Thee!
Thou wast sore stricken of Thy God;
There's not one stroke for me.
Thy tears, Thy blood, beneath it flowed,
Thy bruising healeth me.

Jehovah bade his sword awake;
O Christ, it woke 'gainst Thee!
Thy blood the flaming blade must slake,
Thy heart its sheath must be;
All for my sake my peace to make,
Now sleeps that sword for me.[4]

The Gospel of Propitiation

Let us therefore take a plunge into the meaning of the word *propitiation* in Scripture. It is a neglected word, and one little appreciated in most churches today. But without an understanding of it, our gospel loses much of its power.

In his book *Knowing God,* J. I. Packer devotes a chapter to the importance of propitiation.[5] He reminds us of the Achaian general Agamemnon in Homer's *Iliad,* the classical Greek epic. Agamemnon sets out to recover the lovely Helen, whom Prince Paris had captured and taken to Troy. When things go badly for the Greeks, Agamemnon sends for his own daughter and sacrifices her to appease his gods and to placate their anger, for he sees that they have heartlessly turned their backs on him.

Heathen gods are like that—fickle, subject to changing moods. They are no gods, as I continue to insist, but fallen angelic beings whose brutality and viciousness account for the chaos in the world we live in.

Bible translations that are nervous about their theology avoid the term *propitiation* in such passages as Romans 3:25, Hebrews 2:17, 1 John 2:2 and 4:8-10. I can understand the nervousness, for on one occasion I sat on a committee overseeing the translation of the New Testament into a tribal language. What problems we faced! It is amazing what theological questions arise when you have to choose a particular word and reject another. The (American) Revised Standard Version and the (British) New English Bible both use the term *expiation* in the passages cited above. So what is the difference between expiation and propitiation? Am I not being picky? Well, if I am, I'm in very good company. Actually there is a good deal of difference between expiation and propitiation. Propitiation includes expiation but goes much further.

The idea behind the word *expiation* is that God (who has gentle, kindly feelings toward all of us) is angry about sin, not angry at us. A theologian named C. H. Dodd spent half a book making that point.

John Stott asks the question, "Does God then get angry? If so, then can offerings or rituals assuage his anger? Does he accept bribes? Such concepts seem more pagan than Christian." Stott is clear on the point, however. God is an angry God as well as a tender, loving God. He is angry with the wicked every day (Ps 7:11). And God has a right to be angry with us. Stott goes on to explain that "what is revealed to us in Scripture is a pure doctrine (from which all pagan vulgarities have been expunged) of God's holy wrath, his loving self-sacrifice in Christ to avert his own anger. It is obvious that 'wrath' and 'propitiation' (the placating of wrath) go together."[6]

God does well to be angry the way the world is, and with us as we are. Only his patience and longsuffering hold back his terrible, holy wrath and the judgment he is now about to unleash on the earth. Such gospel matters as reconciliation, justification, pardon for guilty sinners are bound up together with propitiation—appeasing an angry God. As Packer puts it: "The basic description of the saving death of Christ in the Bible is as a *propitiation*, that is, as that which quenched God's wrath against us by obliterating our sins from his sight. God's wrath is his righteousness reacting against unrighteousness; it shows itself in retributive justice."[7]

To propitiate means to placate the wrath of an angry God. Jealousy produces anger—in this case toward a humanity that ignores their Creator and worships other gods who will not love them or treat them with compassion and kindness. Remember, in a marriage relationship, love that lacks any jealous component is defective love. So God was angry, and something had to be done to placate that anger.

But somehow, because pagan gods demanded the same blood

sacrifices that the true God had to use, they compounded their rebellion with a new insult. So all humankind faces the wrath of an angry God.

Still, some people feel that the idea of *placating* divine anger is too pagan a concept. It is fallen angelic beings that demand sacrifice; and how can God do something pagan? But the fallen angels *got the idea from their Creator in the first place.*

Glory with Rage

In God's holy love resides his glory. Manifestations of that glory will, I believe, shortly became commonplace. It has been so in the past and is about to become so again.

It can be deadly dangerous to feel that holy things are commonplace. According to Old Testament ritual law, the Hebrew high priest was to go into the temple's holiest place only once a year, and then only when protected by blood. Was the protection merely symbolic and nothing more? Did the blood of an animal not really protect? Could the priest have omitted the blood and still been safe? Absolutely not!

The people of Beth Shemesh learned about holy things through tragedy as the ark of the covenant came back to them from the Philistines. It had always been kept in the holiest place of all in the tabernacle, but Israel had begun to treat God as a piece of magic that brought them victory. It proved a terrible mistake. I believe that chapters 4, 5 and 6 of 1 Samuel represent absolute historical accuracy. Every phase of what happens in those chapters reflects the danger of carelessly disregarding God's holy love. To sinful human beings, God's love is a very dangerous love.

> God struck down some of the men of Beth Shemesh, putting seventy of them to death because they had looked into the ark of the LORD. The people mourned because of the heavy blow the LORD had dealt them, and the men of Beth Shemesh asked, "Who can stand in the presence of the LORD, this holy God? To whom will the ark go up from here?" (1 Sam 6:19-20)

My own first burst of anger and dismay at God came as I read the story of the first attempt to bring the ark back to Jerusalem. It was carried on an oxcart. "When they came to the threshing floor of Kidon, Uzzah reached out his hand to steady the ark, because the oxen stumbled.

The LORD's anger burned against Uzzah, and he struck him down because he had put his hand on the ark. So he died there before God" (1 Chron 13:9-10).

Reading this story, I was angry, and I was afraid. Tremblingly I told God that I didn't know whether I wanted him to be my God. The kind of God who kills a man, perhaps a family man, simply because he tried to protect the ark from falling was not the kind of God I liked. All I could think of was that King David and the other Israelites had been doing their best and rejoicing over the return of the ark. It never occurred to me that Uzzah might have thought of the ark as a box—a very powerful magical box perhaps, but the box of a God who could not look after himself.[8]

Is God Cruel?

For the secret power of lawlessness is already at work; but the one who now holds it back will continue to do so till he is taken out of the way. And then the lawless one will be revealed, whom the Lord Jesus will overthrow with the breath of his mouth and destroy by the splendor of his coming. (2 Thess 2:7-8)

Evil is mysterious. Everyone is aware of it, but nobody seems able to defeat it. We redefine it to keep pace with its growth, only to realize we fool only ourselves. It is here, horrible and untamable. Law cannot legislate it, prisons cannot contain it, nor can sociologists and psychologists cure it. At present the church seems helpless before it.

Evil is a "he," or a "they," not an "it." But it is to be revealed, to become naked and clear. Paul tells us that a curtain is to be torn aside and Satan revealed. In the same way, Christ is to be revealed and to overthrow Satan and all his works publicly.

Was Calvary unnecessarily cruel? God knew exactly what would happen. On the cross Christ became the sacrificial lamb. Father, Son and Spirit—three persons in one God—were united in their desire that the sacrifice take place. The Son embraced the cross with joy, knowing that death could not hold him, even though its pains would crush him. His greatness is seen in his behavior during his crucifixion. His cry of agony was real. It was the reality of being pierced by his own Father's sword. Love to me and a plunging sword for my Savior. What we often fail to realize is that God not only loved us, *but loved his Son even more.*

But he who died as a lamb rose as King and Conqueror. He had defeated death, Satan and hell and made a mockery of all three. He knew things that evil powers had no knowledge of.

In the early church there were two images that filled the minds of the Christians: the slain Lamb and the mighty Conqueror. This imagery has always filled Christian hymnology, and it preceded the theology of the atonement. It is important that when we look at the cross we keep both images in mind, lest we be overwhelmed with morbidity and sentimentality.

Danger Today?

Our danger lies in assuming that for Christians the peril of God's love has been overcome by the death and resurrection of Christ. It has not. There is still grave danger in treating sacred things lightly. After all, what happened to Ananias and Sapphira (Acts 5:1-11)? God did not excuse their wrongdoing. Indeed, he clearly expected a higher standard of behavior and attitude from those who had been enlightened to divine truth.

It is quite true that God's love is the most self-giving love. It has redeemed us and has already imparted to us a sanctification and a righteousness that could never be won by law. But we cannot ever take it for granted. Our souls may be saved, but our physical lives can be endangered if we grow careless about the holiness of divine things.

This morning I had a telephone call from Hawaii. A member of a growing church there had tried to use *chi* or *ki* (the martial arts form of Hai-chi) in order to heal people. *Chi* is the Chinese form of this particular martial arts discipline, *ki* the Japanese. *Chi* or *ki* is the power within that the practitioner seeks to draw out. Such "soul power" can be demonic. Having watched a spiritually anointed healer, the church member had lusted for the same power. When he understood what he was doing, he repented. But later, as he lay ill in the hospital, his lust for power got the better of him, and he accepted an "anointed" touch from someone in the hospital who was into occult practices. Knowing this, an elder in his church prayed, "Oh Lord, preserve him from this error, *and take him home with you if it is necessary!*"

The man died, still in the hospital, some days later. Coincidence? Perhaps. But in those periods when God's power and glory are manifest on earth, his jealousy for our exclusive love will not tolerate the worship of foreign gods. When an attempt to draw on "inner power" becomes an attempt to use demonic power, as in the Hawaiian man's case, we come into danger. And we are also in grave danger when we worship other gods.

Thus it is always God's people who are in the greatest physical danger of too close a contact with the burning and holy love. Hence Paul's words to the Corinthian church warning them not to be careless about the eucharistic elements or about God's presence at the Lord's Supper: *"That is why many among you are weak and sick, and a number of you have fallen asleep"* (1 Cor 11:30).

The means by which God reaches out to us in holy love can be the cause of our physical deaths. It happened in the days of the Acts of the Apostles. It will happen again. For the unsaved, of course, there is the far greater danger of hell. Those of us who are saved will at least be "saved, but only as one escaping through the flames" (1 Cor 3:15). But we must think of the lost, for whom we have received a sacred commission.

"Fly from the Wrath to Come!"

John Bunyan is describing himself when he depicts Christian in *The Pilgrim's Progress*. Weeping and praying day and night, Christian has succeeded only in irritating his family and neighbors. In the end, he is despairing and "walking in the fields . . . (as he was wont) reading in his book," moaning and crying out loudly. Christian describes himself as condemned to die, and after that to come to judgment, "and I find I am not willing to do the first, nor able to do the second." As Paul Robson would have expressed it, he is "tired of living, and scared of dying."

Such weariness of life again begins to affect many in our day. Such fear of death is about to break across the whole world. In Bunyan's story it is at this point that Mr. Evangelist advises Christian to "fly from the wrath to come."[9] And when you do that, you fly in the direction of the pathway of holiness, drawn by a loving God.

John Bunyan knew the terror of divine wrath. Yet it was precisely such a fear that made Bunyan the flame that he subsequently became. To experience both the terror and the tenderness of God makes for a real evangelist with a tender, terror-filled presentation of the gospel. Today's church has lost all sense of God's wrath. We need a further dose—and a good one—of Bunyan's terror of God and of God's tenderness toward us.[10]

But there is the pull of God himself in all of us, the pull of love as well as the flight from terror. And it is God's love that matters.

God's Side of the Gospel and Ours

The other day I listened to Mohsen Demian, an Egyptian surgeon, as he gave an impassioned plea. Demian wanted his hearers to see the gospel drama from God's point of view. One side of the gospel story concerns the Son of God, who in loving obedience to the Father came to the world to save sinners. To do so he became a human being, declared the kingdom's nature, was persecuted and crucified. He had come to conquer sin, death and Satan in order to secure our redemption. The proof of his shattering blow to the kingdom of Satan was that he rose from the dead and ascended to glory, from whence he rules the universe while we await his return in power.

This is the side of the gospel with which we are familiar, but it is only one side. For the gospel is not about us, but about *him*—God. It is the drama of a Father who seeks a bride for his Son. But the bride's garments are filthy. She is at present an unclean, stinking whore. We like to speak of her being "pure" already, in the sense of being cleansed by the blood of the Son. And this is true. But it is not enough. Jesus' bride is to be "a radiant church, without stain or wrinkle or any other blemish, but holy and blameless" (Eph 5:27). At present she is anything but that.

This is the side of the gospel drama that Mohsen presented with such passion. God's side of the drama is of infinitely greater consequence than our own side. When we glory in one side and forget the other, we preach a humanity-centered gospel. The gospel is primarily about the nature of God. *It is about him.*

Angry and jealous though God may be, he is determined to create a bride worthy of his Son—the son of the Father. And he will do so, perhaps very soon. We have yet to see him move both in judgment and in loving power in the way he is capable of moving. He will do what he has determined, not just for our sakes, but for the glory and satisfaction of the Son.

This is why I write about the pathway of holiness. I encourage you to walk in it—both in personal holiness and in the corporate holiness of the church, the bride of Christ.

2

SCRIPTURE
TRUTH AS
A GUIDE TO
HOLINESS

Then you will know the truth,
and the truth will
set you free. (John 8:32)

Buy the truth and do not sell it;
get wisdom, discipline and
understanding. (Proverbs 23:23)

*I*F YOU WERE TO ASK CHRISTIANS FROM A DOZEN DIFFERENT DENOMINA-
tions, "How can I get to be holy?" you might get a dozen different
answers. Two or three of them could be contradictory. Priests and
pastors are trained in different seminaries, and their theologies generally
reflect the seminaries where they have been trained. When they were
students, they found themselves trusting and respecting certain teachers
and accepted what those teachers taught. Jack Deere says,

> The truth is, if you take a student who has no position on the
> millennium and send him to Westminster Seminary, he will probably
> come out an amillennialist. If you take the same student and send
> him to Dallas Seminary, he is even more likely to come out a
> premillennialist. There will be few exceptions to this rule. Our
> environment, our theological traditions, and our teachers have much
> more to do with what we believe than we realize. In some cases
> they have much more influence over what we believe than the Bible
> itself.[1]

"Wait a minute," you say. "You're really talking about controversial
doctrines. We're talking about something simple and major—holiness.
There would never be such disagreement over major biblical truths."
But every major doctrine is or has been controversial. John Piper,
himself a biblical scholar, says, "Can controversial teachings nurture

Christlikeness? Before you answer this question, ask another one: Are there any significant biblical teachings that have not been controversial? I cannot think of even one."[2]

Cedric B. Johnson, a Christian psychologist, makes the same point: One biblical commentary will persuade me to accept covenant theology with its practice of infant baptism. Another erudite scholar seeks to persuade me that baptism is for believers only. Historically, churches split over the day of worship, the ordination of women, integration, and the use of musical instruments in worship. Today we seek biblically informed answers to equally difficult questions, such as nuclear war, homosexuality,[3] genetic engineering, and divorce.[4]

How to Recognize Truth

So—is it possible to be sure of the truth about holiness *from my own search of the Scripture?* If Piper and Johnson are correct—if every major doctrine is or has been controversial, confused and shrouded in disagreement—where can I, personally, find reliable information? Can I ever know the truth, even from Scripture? And—terrible thought—is even my own church right in everything it teaches?[5]

What *is* the teaching of the apostles? It is precisely here that the debate becomes the fiercest. Let me say at once that Scripture must always be primary. And we must never say that we have received such a powerful anointing from God that we do not need scholars. No, no. We need every bit of help we can get. But the trouble is that each one of us struggles to live the kind of life God calls us to. Our basic problem is, How do I get free from the sins I struggle against? While the struggle will, I believe, last as long as we live, there can be real progress. Individual sins can be overcome one by one.

In this book I will share my own heart, my own experience. Among these experiences I have had visions. I do not record them to convince anybody, because visions can be false visions. I just want you to know where my thoughts come from. Scripture offers both a prophetic and an apostolic example for doing this sort of thing. Therefore though I could be accused of writing a book that has more to do with me than with Scripture, I will run that risk. Your experience may well be quite different. The common thread lies in a God who cares for us all and who is interested in all we do.

Our lives are like tangled pieces of string. Your tangle differs from mine. But the same Christ has done a sufficient work for both of us. Though there may be a basic approach to untangling string—fundamental principles you watch out for—*no two pieces of string get untangled in quite the same way.* Our stories will differ in their details. The order in which God will tackle certain sins may differ. So I share my experiences and myself—even poking fun at myself at times.

The test of whether we are "onto" truth is whether we are being set free from sinful tendencies that once defeated us. Most of us are not free—but let me phrase that more positively: most of us, I hope, are progressing along a pathway to freedom. Our sanctification is in process. We are like a bumper sticker I once saw which pleaded, "Be patient. God isn't finished with me yet."

The Personal Nature of Truth

Truth is personal. That is to say, it is found in a person and involves an ongoing dynamic relationship with that person. "I am the way and the truth and the life," Jesus once said (Jn 14:6). Jesus is the truth about God. Knowledge of him is knowledge of God. Such knowledge does not come from a course of instruction (though courses of instruction can be helpful) but from a lifetime of personal relationship. Truth is not discovered in a series of abstractions so much as in an ongoing relationship with God himself.

Messiah Jesus is the truth. Truth is "not hard to understand, *though it is often very hard to accept.*"[6] To know Christ, to walk in his fellowship, is the key to truth. Such a relationship can be devastating to one's ego. J. I. Packer, in the third chapter of his book *Knowing God,* says, "As you listen to what God is saying, you find yourself brought very low; for God talks to you about your sin, and guilt, and weakness, and blindness, and folly, and compels you to judge yourself hopeless and helpless, and to cry out for forgiveness."[7]

Yet devastation, personal devastation of this kind, is necessary if holiness is to grow. Relationship has to do with the totality of our being, with body, mind and spirit, with intellect, will, emotions—in a word, with all that makes us human. In Scripture "all that makes us human" is called *the heart*. Christianity is not a mere intellectual proposition, even though it may be propositional. A doorway must therefore be opened between head and "heart" (in the biblical sense). Richard Baxter tells us: "What excellency would there be in much learning and knowledge, if the obstructions between the head and the heart were but opened, and the affections did but correspond to the understanding."[8]

Mercifully, a personal relationship with Christ does not only devastate. It also provides profound and indescribable reassurance. Packer is clear about this.

> You come to realize as you listen that God is actually opening his heart to you, making friends with you and enlisting you as a colleague—in Barth's phrase, a covenant partner. It is a staggering thing, but it is true—the relationship in which sinful human beings know God is one in which God, so to speak, takes them on to his staff, to be henceforth his fellow workers (see 1 Cor 3:9) and personal friends.[9]

Friendship with Christ is a means to holiness. Courses in Bible knowledge can always help, but there is no substitute for a personal relationship with Christ. As he teaches you, he gives freedom. So if truth does not free you from sin, you do not know truth. You are merely parroting it verbally. Truth frees.

Jeremiah and Self-Deception

Holiness arises out of scriptural truth. But we can twist scriptural truth to make it mean what we want. Then we become proud of our knowledge, and pride exposes us to the powers of darkness. For this reason Jeremiah had a problem with the Bible scholars of his day—or rather, God had.

> How can you say, "We are wise,
>   for we have the law of the LORD,"
> when actually the lying pen of the scribes
>   has handled it falsely? (Jer 8:8)

These words are from the text of a speech God is giving Jeremiah. He wants him to deliver the speech before the Israelites of his day. It has to do (among other things) with avoiding the dangers of scholarship. The scribes were scholars. They could read and write when most people could not. Their job was to copy outworn texts of the five books of Moses, as well as other books and documents.

The words of the speech are shocking. God calls what certain men write in his name *lies*. Scribes are handling his word *falsely*. They have copied the words of Scripture accurately enough, but they are adding their own comments—written or oral—on the meaning of the text. (Presumably the Talmud, a collection of Jewish tradition and commentaries which dates back to around A.D. 200, well after Jeremiah's day, had forerunners in some form.) Jeremiah refers to the scribes' comments, written or oral, as lies.

God had chosen Israel as his people. He had given them his Word from Mount Sinai. The Israelites had a unique destiny among the nations. Yet God sees them as unwise and their "biblical" arguments as stupid. To have words from Sinai is evidently not enough.

Now, if truth is meant to set a person free, then you can claim to have the truth only when you walk in freedom—freedom from sins that once enslaved you. Wisdom does not consist in having Scripture, but in having discovered what sets you free. "We are wise," God's people mistakenly proclaimed, "because we have the law of the Lord." We do the same. *Having* the Word does not make us wise.

The Scribe's Temptation

Am I attacking scholarship? Absolutely not! We need scholarship, but must be aware of its dangers. Scholarship can make us proud, for "knowledge puffs up, but love builds up" (1 Cor 8:1).

The proudest scribe would never have denied that Moses had received words from God. The scribes believed so far as possessing and copying the Scriptures was concerned. Hence their obsession with absolute accuracy. But there can be a sort of schizophrenic approach to Scripture, a disease to which scribelike scholars are especially vulnerable.

Suppose that a certain scribe (we'll call him Jeconiah) is copying Leviticus 18 from an old scroll to a new one for the fifth time. He comes across the words now found in verse 16: "Do not have sexual relations with your brother's wife; that would dishonor your brother." The last time he copied those same words, he had just begun an affair with his sister-in-law. He had put his pen down, troubled. In the end he had decided to confess his sin and make the appropriate sin offering. After that things had gone well for a while—until for one reason or another, the affair started up again.

Now he faces the same words. He has to copy them, word by word, accurately. (Try doing it yourself with a favorite chapter. You will be surprised at the impact the words have on you!)

What happens to Jeconiah at this point? A number of possibilities present themselves. What he does will depend partly on what sort of person he is. He might, for instance, repeat what he did last time, only this time the affair with his sister-in-law might recommence sooner. Perhaps he might begin to despair. He could harden his heart and say in the appropriate Hebrew words, "Oh, what the heck!" In this case he would begin the process of searing his conscience with a hot iron (1 Tim 4:2).

On the other hand, suppose he did something else. He could decide that the words he was copying did not apply to him, or that they did not exactly mean what they say. He could say (again in the appropriate phraseology of the day), "Nobody can be that pure in practice! It's just a standard we gotta aim at! It's trying that matters!" He could even develop very good arguments to show that the words he has just copied mean the exact opposite of what they say. And in all these ways, without realizing he was doing so, he would profoundly change his attitude both to Scripture and (more important) to the Lord of Scripture.

Human nature has not changed. Today we are merely what our imaginary Jeconiah was centuries ago. At every level, from our first tentative steps in Bible reading to wrestling with advanced textual studies, we face a standard hazard of biblical scholarship. We approach interpretation with psychological weighting of which we are often unconscious. Jeconiah could be driven into untruth by spiritual, moral and psychological forces beyond his ken. The sad thing is that he might never know it.

This is why the only real test of whether you know the truth is whether you walk in progressive freedom from sins that once had brought you down again and again.

Let's say Jeconiah decides to go on puzzling about the Torah (what he would call the books of Moses). Obviously, meaning is important. It becomes his chief concern, so that he is obsessed with it. Years later when he is an old man, widely respected in his community, someone approaches him with a problem.

"Doesn't Torah say _____?"

"Strange you should ask. As a matter of fact it doesn't say *that* exactly. What it does say is _____, and what it really means is _____."

By this time Jeconiah's conscience is thoroughly hardened.

The Scribes' Shame

Jeremiah had not finished the speech I started to quote. He went on to talk about the sort of pride of which we still stand in danger:

The "wise" [my quotation marks] will be put to shame;
>   they will be dismayed and trapped.
Since they have rejected the word of the LORD,
>   what kind of wisdom do they have? (Jer 8:9)

Notice: the scribes are seen as *rejecting* God's Word. Holiness arises from a knowledge of God and a heart relationship with him. Knowledge of God comes through studying, meditating on and praying over Scripture's impact on my life. Translators have done a good job in giving us the Scriptures. Yet expertise alone is not enough. The scribes said they were *interpreting God's Word correctly*, yet it did not change their lives.

There is danger for all of us, for in a sense all of us are scholars—we read and interpret the Scriptures for ourselves. Again and again pride raises its head, whatever our level or type of scholarship may be. It emerges in the Gospels, in those who opposed Christ's own ministry. The same prideful opposition plagued Paul throughout his. And pride appears in the different and competing Bible translations.

Of certain scholars God asks in scorn: What kind of wisdom do they think they have? Paul describes it as a form of knowledge, but not the truth. In other words, the old scribe we pictured earlier could display "zeal for God," but zeal that was not "based on knowledge" (Rom 10:2). In the early centuries of the Christian church the Gnostics exalted knowledge above faith. Gnosticism is not dead in today's church. Nor is arid evangelical intellectualism.

I suppose in this life we will never be free from some sin that plagues us. But there should be in all our lives a steady progression. To walk in truth is to walk in ever-greater freedom from sin. We struggle—or, in despair, give up struggling—against sinful habits that dog our Christian walk. From these, little by little, Christ would set us free.

If we struggle vainly against sin, let us cry out to God. It is sure evidence that at some point we still walk in darkness, and that God is trying to get through to us. We may have to go on crying out. But God will eventually show us where we are amiss.

Finding the Truth That Frees

John Bunyan was a problem-plagued tinker of dubious morality. Yet he became one of the greatest English allegorists and a powerful minister of the gospel. Gifford was John Bunyan's pastor and teacher. He appears as Evangelist in Bunyan's *Pilgrim's Progress*. Gifford made the point that until the Holy Ghost reveals a Scripture truth to us, we may "understand" the truth, but not well enough for it to deliver us from a particular sin. Pride prevents us from understanding truth, from hearing the Spirit: "For, when temptation comes strongly upon you, if you have not received these things with evidence from heaven, you will soon find that you do not have that help and strength to resist that you thought you did."[10]

Notice the words "if you have not received these things with evidence from heaven." Gifford is speaking of the way the Holy Spirit *reveals* Scriptures to us. God makes the words come alive. So it is that at certain points we find ourselves marveling, *I've read that repeatedly, yet only now do I see what it is saying.*

According to Gifford, the acid test of divinely imparted truth was that it strengthened the believer against temptation. Bunyan was profoundly impressed by what Gifford told him. Only truth that the Spirit reveals to the individual soul does this. Bunyan says:

This was just what my soul needed. I had found out by sad experience the truth of these words. So I prayed to God that in nothing related to his glory and my own eternal happiness would I be without the confirmation from heaven that I needed. I clearly saw the difference between human notions and revelation from God.[11] Think of the ancient scholars, the scribes of Jeremiah's day. They copied the sacred books accurately. Every word was precious. Every word mattered. Jesus talks about "jots" and "tittles." "I tell you the truth," he once said, "until heaven and earth disappear, not the smallest letter, not the least stroke of a pen, will by any means disappear from the Law until everything is accomplished" (Mt 5:18).

Truth is of inestimable importance. Yet truth needs to do its work. Truth alone can free you. But freedom can elude you. Scripture is the heart of truth about God and about how we may relate to him, but there needs to be some sort of connection between you and the truth that frees—some spark to bring life.

God wants to give you this spark. Ask him for it. Ask him to show you the thing he wants to show you. Remember the tangled piece of string. There is an order in which God wants to deal with *your* sins. If you feel you are getting nowhere, don't give up. Call on him again and again. But *listen*. Expect him to speak, especially through the Scriptures. You want to be holy; he wants you to be holy. He wants to connect with you more than you do.

But let me get back to the issue of pride in our knowledge. Pride tells us that we are not absolutely helpless. But when it comes to holiness, we *are* helpless. You can no more get rid of sins in your life than you can fly to the moon. Recognizing your helplessness is the first step to holiness, and pride stands in the way. Pride is such an important obstacle that I devote the next chapter to it.

3

DELIVERANCE FROM THE DARKNESS OF PRIDE

Your heart became proud
on account of your beauty,
and you corrupted your wisdom
because of your splendor.
So I threw you to the earth;
I made a spectacle of you . . . (Ezekiel 28:17)

When I survey the wondrous Cross,
On which the Prince of Glory died,
My richest gain I count but loss
And pour contempt on all my pride. (Isaac Watts)

The condemnation of God by man is not based on the truth,
but on arrogance, on an underhanded conspiracy.
(Pope John Paul II, Crossing the Threshold of Hope*)*

*T*HE POPE IS RIGHT. WE HUMAN BEINGS, IN OUR PRIDE, PUT GOD IN THE
wrong. We do it all the time, justifying ourselves in the face of God and
of God's Scripture. In my case arrogance and pride began early. They
were present in the seed of my parents.

Because we are probably all similar, let me describe some of my
earliest fantasies. They may ring a bell for you. I used to have imaginary
companions—a psychological symptom generally attributed to loneliness. But my question is, Why did my lonely fantasies take the particular
form they took?

One of my imaginary companions was an Eskimo boy my own age.
He would complain of the heat to me. "You call this *hot?*" I would ask
him in the astonishment of conscious superiority. "This isn't hot at all.
Personally, I feel like shivering."

I had similar conversations, but about the cold, with another
imaginary friend from tropical Africa. My object was to impress my
companions by my superiority. To my northern friend I boasted of
insensitivity to heat, to the other of insensitivity to cold. In both cases
I gained delight in the imaginary worship and admiration of imaginary
boys, by their awestruck adoration of me. Psychological "reasons" (such

as loneliness) did not make what I was doing any less dangerous, any less sinful.

Sin is like cancer, and cancer kills kids faster than it kills adults. For in our pride, we not only put God in the wrong but actually desire to take his place, to enjoy the worship that is rightly his. Whatever form the thing takes, it is detected readily at a fantasy level—just check your thought stream or old diaries, and especially old prayer journals.

Pride and Pride

Let me begin by distinguishing certain good things from pride—things that can be confused with it. For instance, wanting praise and taking pleasure in being praised is not necessarily pride. How could our ambition to receive Christ's praise—"Well done, good and faithful servant!"—be anything but virtuous? When I used to seek the admiration of imaginary companions as a child, I was seeking not praise but *worship*. I wanted to elicit admiration, awe, wonder! I wanted to impress—to stun an admirer. Even imaginary awe was better than none. This is precisely why Satan fell. He wanted the worship that belongs to God alone. The applause given to prima donnas and prima ballerinas can awaken a lust for adoration. Christian artists and preachers—beware!

But let me get back to my point about good things that can be confused with pride. To love one's country is good. Loyalty to one's country (as distinct from patriotism) is not a form of pride. By all means love your country, your nation. Be loyal. Love the people of your own nation. Of course, loyal Christians will want their nation to know about Jesus. Throughout history, this sort of commitment has gotten many Christians imprisoned and martyred. Loyalty seeks the best for one's countrymen. But patriotism, a very different attitude, says, "My country—right *or wrong!*"

Pride in one's own children is not necessarily pride in the bad sense, though it can be. We can be grateful for our children and proud of them so long as our rejoicing is not a feeling of superiority toward people whose children struggle in school or have gone wrong in some way. In other words, God did not give us children to prove our superiority over other parents.

God taught me this lesson during the long delay between our firstborn and subsequent children. My wife and I were older, and in a hurry. Disturbed by the delay, I knelt one day to pray in a park in Paris, when there were few people around. I asked God for another son with the caveat "if he will live to your glory."

Quite distinctly the Holy Spirit said, "To *my* glory, or to *yours?*"

I was shaken a little. Then came, "What about me and Adam?"

At first perplexed, I began to realize that at the time of creation God had known of all the wars, the cruelty, the diseases, the terrible tragedies that would follow the entry of Satanic pride into human history. Yet he still had given Adam life. Was he asking me to do something similar?

I asked, "What d'you mean?"

Immediately into my mind came a picture of the walls of a prison not far from the home of my childhood. I felt sick.

"You mean he would go to jail?" The possibility of having a son who would go to jail frightened me. I could feel moisture penetrating my trouser knees. But I did not rise. I knew that I was being offered a son who would go to jail. I also knew I could refuse that son. Perhaps someone else would have him. I have no idea how a sovereign God works this sort of thing. But there was no answer to my feeling of panic, only silence.

Finally, rather shaken, I said, "OK. I'll have him!"

Two months later our second son was conceived. By that time I had forgotten the prayer "conversation." My dialogue with God did not lead to a sort of self-fulfilling prophecy. I gradually forgot about it, and recalled it only much later when the clear differences between Kevin and our other children became so obvious that they could no longer be ignored.

A nightmare began then. Did God *cause* my second son to sin? Obviously not. But he had known what would happen. And he had given me a choice.

Later came two prophecies, both from men with established reputations for accurate prophecy. A cloud of darkness rested on that particular son. At some date in the future it would be snatched from above his head, and he would change. In the meantime Kevin never lost his longing for the things of God. In jail he would organize Bible studies. He would lay his hands on other prisoners, and these would occasionally fall on the ground, overwhelmed by the Spirit of God. How does one explain such things?

Kevin did change, and quite suddenly. But first I had to understand that children are not necessarily given to us so that they might contribute to our sense of superiority. God gives us children so that we can boast not of them, but of himself—and there is a difference.

The Dangers of Knowledge

Scripture was given to make us holy—fit for God's presence, for fellowship *with* him and use *by* him. But the study of Scripture (like any other form of study) can make us secretly proud of what we know. It can therefore have the opposite effect. Let me go further. Even "spiritual" activity, like meditation on Scripture—even the much-vaunted journaling—can make us proud. Anything can wind up revealing our arrogance.

Years ago I wrote what follows in one of my journals:

Recently I began to find it was harder to write down my thoughts. I was ashamed of what I discovered inside me. What should have been addressed to you was directed to an imaginary reader, reading over my shoulder. I fight against the tendency [to impress my imaginary reader] but find the habit almost impossible to overcome. Five minutes later, I'm doing the same thing, "playing to the gallery" as it were.

I was guilty of subtle self-flattery, about which Philip Dodderidge has something to say. Speaking of our inner evasions of conviction, he writes, "Yet I know the treachery, and the self flattery of a sinful and corrupted heart."[1]

Without realizing what I was after, I wanted to be worshiped; and to seek worship is to seek Satanic pride. God showed me that absorption with him brings escape from our pride. Pride craves glory. Only one person can be trusted with glory, with universal worship and adoration, and that person is a threesome—the triune God. He alone can be trusted with adoration. When we render it to him, *he shares that same glory with us—placing glory on us, as it were*. The effect of imparted glory is to take away our awareness of ourselves. We become too preoccupied with his glory to be aware of our own. When God shares his glory with his people, it creates the only truly healthy "mutual admiration society."

C. S. Lewis makes the statement that pride was what made Satan the devil. If this is so, it is important. Many scholars see certain verses in Ezekiel 28 as more than a prophecy directed at the king of Tyre, as a reference to Satan and the cause of his fall from heaven:

You were the model of perfection,
> full of wisdom and perfect in beauty.

You were in Eden,
> the garden of God;

every precious stone adorned you:
> ruby, topaz and emerald,
> chrysolite, onyx and jasper,
> sapphire, turquoise and beryl.

Your settings and mountings were made of gold;
> on the day you were created they were prepared.

You were anointed as a guardian cherub,
> for so I ordained you.

You were on the holy mount of God;
> you walked among the fiery stones. . . .

Your heart became proud
> on account of your beauty,

and you corrupted your wisdom
> because of your splendor. (vv. 12-14, 17)

It follows that pride must be the very heart of evil, the quintessence of rebellion against God. Pride gives rise to every other evil. It is the source of "the works of the flesh" and is incompatible with all the fruit of the Spirit (Gal 5:19-23). At every point it militates against the beatitudes (Mt 5:3-10).

Where are the people described in the Sermon on the Mount? Years ago Tozer wrote words that are still true of the church: "Instead of poverty of spirit we find the rankest kind of pride; instead of mourners we find pleasure seekers; instead of meekness, arrogance; instead of hunger after righteousness we hear men saying, 'I am rich and increased with goods and have need of nothing'; instead of mercy we find cruelty."[2]

Facing the insidious effects and the ubiquitous presence of pride in our own lives will begin to teach us what personal holiness is about. Pride, the root of all sin, has its origin in our foreparents and is now in us.

When Satan tempted Eve, it was to pride that he tempted her. "You will be like God," he told her. That was a heady prospect. In that moment Satan successfully implanted pride in Eve, and pride entered the human race. "Pride leads to every other vice: it is the complete anti-God state of mind."[3]

Isaiah proclaims divine indignation against all that leads to vanity and pride. It will be a stench in God's nostrils and will call for judgment. In the third chapter of his prophecy he says,

The LORD says,
"The women of Zion are haughty,
walking along with outstretched necks,
flirting with their eyes,
tripping along with mincing steps,
with ornaments jingling on their ankles. . . .
Instead of fragrance there will be a stench. . . .
Your men will fall by the sword,
your warriors in battle." (vv. 16, 24-25)

The psalmist tells us God detects a proud person from a long way away: "the proud he knows from afar" (Ps 138:6). Isaiah talked about a stench or a stink. Is the psalmist saying that God *smells* the pride in us and wrinkles his nose? If so, does he also detect the aroma of humility from the far reaches of the throne room?

More Consequences of Pride

There is a sequence in Proverbs 6 which may or may not be deliberate. Yet it raises again in my mind the horrible consequences of pride.

There are six things the LORD hates,
seven that are detestable to him:
haughty eyes,
a lying tongue,

> hands that shed innocent blood,
> a heart that devises wicked schemes,
> feet that are quick to rush into evil,
> a false witness who pours out lies
> and a man who stirs up dissension among brothers. (Prov 6:16-19)

Haughty eyes are the eyes of a proud and arrogant person. I have to plead guilty to the condition at times. In an argument, being right is very important to me. Sometimes I have caught myself at the point of lying to win an argument. You couldn't call what I was about to say a lie, perhaps. It would depend on your definition. But I can shade the truth to win a point. Pride leads to lying.

Once I was with a group of surgeons and a psychiatric colleague. My colleague was encouraging the surgeons to tell dirty jokes. He did so to tease me and subsequently to embarrass them. Once they had begun to be themselves, my colleague laughed and said, "John here is a minister. I hope you realize how he feels about the stories you guys are telling!"

One of the men blushed. Then, turning on me, my colleague asked, "But John, you don't really believe in all that stuff in the Old Testament about the Garden of Eden, do you?"

I felt ashamed and said, "Well not exactly." Later I could not let the matter rest and made it plain that yes, I did believe what Scripture says. Why had I been ashamed? Because pride rose up within me. I did not want to look like a fool. Haughty eyes and a lying tongue go together.

Experience will show that they go together with "hands that shed innocent blood." Perhaps not immediately, but there is an evolution in evil which will eventually wind up in promiscuous and careless indifference to killing. This is the kind of killing that grows more common daily in the streets of large cities. It is so in war. During World War II, when I flew in a dive-bomber, I did not think of enemy ships as containing people, especially people who were personally no more guilty than I. I thought of only two things: my own survival and getting an accurate hit on the ship below. The consequences of the exploding bomb were not my business. I just did not think.

As for a heart that devises wicked schemes, it arises also out of pride. It works this way in local congregations. Pride gives you the "right" to indulge in critical feelings about other church members. You "discuss" the matter with your friends, "as a matter for prayer." Before you know it you are saying, "You know, something ought to be done about this." Thus grow the seeds that result in a pastor's dismissal or some other disciplinary action.

I know that real sin must not be ignored, but Jesus sought to rescue people from sin. He did not come to judge but to save (Jn 12:47). Our whole orientation must be changed if we are to be like our Master and Lord.

The steady deterioration from pride to every form of sin shows that pride is "a package deal." Once you begin with it, there is no telling where you may stop. The original sin gives rise to the rest, and "feet that are quick to rush into evil, a false witness who pours out lies and a man who stirs up dissension among brothers" inevitably follow, as night and day succeed each other.

God's Hatred

There are things *and even people* that seem to merit the hatred of God himself. You don't believe it? Scripture tells us, "The LORD detests all the proud of heart. Be sure of this: They will not go unpunished" (Prov 16:5). God detests not only their sin but the people themselves. Proud people are "an abomination" to him.

We assure ourselves that Jesus never hates, yet he repeatedly curses the Pharisees in Matthew 23. However we may define hatred, we associate it with curses.

When we give way to pride, we walk, as it were, into the region of divine hatred. And it was *pride* in the scribes and Pharisees that Jesus cursed.

> Everything they do is done for men to see: They make their phylacteries wide and the tassels on their garments long; they love the place of honor at banquets and the most important seats in the synagogues; they love to be greeted in the marketplaces and to have men call them "Rabbi." (Mt 23:5)

We are no different from the Pharisees and scribes. The modern vanity is clinging to any "doctor" we have or can name. Name-dropping, for example, has its roots in pride. If you cannot be somebody yourself, you are tempted to boast of people you hobnob with. We want to awaken admiration, awe. In us all is the same sin as the pharisaical love of hearing ourselves called "Rabbi." Those of us who can lay claim to a doctorate of one kind or another are not averse to hearing ourselves addressed as, or referred to, as "Doctor" this-or-that. We may even notice a slight sense of annoyance when someone refers to us mistakenly as "Mr." or "Ms."

Pride is particularly a problem for people who have not lived in open sin, who have been relatively sheltered all their lives. It shows itself when they meet Christians who fall into "real" sin. Pride has many fruits, of which vanity and arrogance are examples.

It would seem that this basic sin, this sin above all others, arouses God's wrath as no other sin does. Pride in our church, pride in our nation, pride in our accomplishments, our wealth, the sort of car we drive or the sort of house we live in, runs the risk of divine anger. It is at this point that Christianity differs most radically from the rest of the world.

There is also something ominous about the threat that proud people "will not go unpunished." Whether the day of wrath is stored up for the future or meted out here and now, the thought that disturbs us is that God does not forget.

Most Scripture references to pride are to the sin itself rather than the person who commits it.

The LORD Almighty has a day in store
    for all the proud and lofty,
    for all that is exalted
    (and they will be humbled),
for all the cedars of Lebanon, tall and lofty,
    and all the oaks of Bashan. . . .
The arrogance of man will be brought low
    and the pride of men humbled;
the LORD alone will be exalted in that day. (Is 2:12-13, 17)

I shudder, gripped by a momentary sense of fear as I read such words. This in spite of knowing what Christ has accomplished.

In all the things we look down on (drunkenness, sexual immorality) there remains some good. In drunkenness there is conviviality and a reaching out to other human beings. Even in immoral sexual behavior there can be a reaching out to someone else—something is being shared. Pride, in contrast, is devoid of anything good.

Even competitiveness, while good to teach us certain virtues, has its dangers. Lewis points out,

Each person's pride is in competition with everyone else's pride. It is because I wanted to be the big noise at the party that I am so annoyed at someone else being the big noise. . . . We say that people are proud of being rich, or clever, or good looking, but they are not. They are proud of being richer, or cleverer, or better looking, than others.[4]

To have a competitive spirit is a sign that we have not yet been "made perfect in love." I smile as I type the words, freely confessing that while the holiness process is going on in me, I am a long way from perfection myself.

There is a terrible, haunting question Lewis asks concerning the dangers we face as we deal with holy things. Because expertise in such things contributes to pride—pride of which we are often unconscious—there is a further danger, and Lewis puts his finger on it: "How is it that people who are quite obviously eaten up with pride can say they believe in God, and appear to themselves very religious? I am afraid it means they are worshipping an imaginary God."[5]

Humility

We contrast pride with humility. Humility does not consist of thinking you are no good, but rather of not thinking of yourself at all. Loving awareness of others begins to dawn as we grow humble. Ego begins to fade. Humble people are not self-conscious. They do not think about themselves, because they know they are pardoned and accepted by God. They almost lose self-awareness, partly because of their awareness of Christ, of his forgiveness and loving acceptance of them. Humble people really are free to get excited and pleased with the triumphs of others. Humble people have been set free to love.

C. S. Lewis expresses it well:

Do not imagine that if you meet a humble man, he will be what most people call "humble" nowadays: he will not be a sort of greasy, smarmy person, who is always telling you that, of course, he is nobody. Probably all you will think about him is that he seemed a cheerful, intelligent chap who took a real interest in what *you* said to *him*. . . . He will not be thinking about humility. He will not be thinking about himself at all.[6]

Proud people, on the other hand, are thinking all the time about themselves. Either they are worrying about what other people think of them, or they are so sure of their superiority that they are indifferent of what other people think—careless of fools and ignorant people. Either way, their thoughts are full of themselves—their inferiority or their superiority.

Pride is self-worship. Humility is to have been set free from self-worship.

God loves humility. Isaiah tells us of his preferences:

I live in a high and holy place,
    but also with him who is contrite and lowly in spirit,
to revive the spirit of the lowly,
    and to revive the heart of the contrite. (Is 57:15)

This is the one I esteem:
    he who is humble and contrite in spirit,
    and trembles at my word. (Is 66:2)

I referred earlier to the Beatitudes, pointing out that they are inimical to pride. Notice who, according to Jesus, are the blessed ones. "Blessed are the poor in spirit. . . . Blessed are those who mourn. . . . Blessed are the meek . . . those who hunger and thirst for righteousness . . . the merciful" (Mt 5:3-7). To be poor in spirit is to recognize your need. You mourn because you recognize it, and you know that God alone can change you. Such is also the character of a meek person. Meek people are not weak people, but they feel no need to be defensive. They listen to God, or even to you, when you tell them what's wrong. God is always right, of course, whereas you may not be. But a truly meek person will not react indignantly or with hostility even when you accuse them wrongly.

Proverbs 3:34 tells us that God "mocks proud mockers but gives grace to the humble." This verse caught the attention of New Testament writers. It is quoted both by Peter (1 Pet 5:5) and by James (Jas 4:6).

Conquering Your Pride

Can pride be conquered? If there is any logic at all in the Christian gospel, then it can be conquered, and the conquest should not be impossibly difficult. However, once you make a serious attempt to overcome your pride, you will discover how very difficult it seems to be. The old saw about being "proud of one's humility" is a ghastly reality. One can ape humility, but the attempt deceives few people.

Part of our problem is that many of us are addicted to other people's opinion of us. We need to be liked, to be accepted. We need to discover Christ's own "secret." Don Williams, a Vineyard pastor, writes of the source of Christ's freedom—his absolute certainty of the love of the Father—and its results: "Being free from people, Jesus was free for people. Common folk gladly listened to him. He could relate to fishermen, revolutionaries, soldiers and slaves. When he went to the home of a Pharisee, he didn't have a problem if he met a prostitute there. He loved to eat with tax collectors and sinners."[7]

How, then, may we be free from pride? I must not exaggerate the ease with which the freedom can come. Satanic pride dies hard. Essentially, we find freedom as Jesus found it, by being secure in the Father's love. Logically, if he loves us, he will never abandon us; he will always watch over us like a mother hawk, flying to our rescue the moment we face danger unawares. It is security in the Father's love that frees us.

You say, "I know all this. This is not a problem for me." Quite so. I do not need to teach you the logical implications of the gospel. You can think for yourself. But there is knowing and *knowing*.

In the next chapter I will mention a vision I had many years ago, during which the different levels of knowing became apparent to me. God had been trying to get the matter across to me for years. Many years before that first vision, I had read in the Song of Songs,

How delightful is your love, my sister, my bride!

How much more pleasing is your love than wine,

and the fragrance of your perfume than any spice! (Song 4:10)

The comparison bewildered me. How could wine be like love? Well, for one thing, you can't really *know* either without experiencing them. Experts on love and marriage who have never been in love or married have a mistaken expertise. And the same is true of drinking. Every Christmas in my home we drank port wine. I was permitted a small glass. When you drank it, it felt good inside. There was a sort of inner glow. Love is the same. You have to drink it to know it.

So far as the love of God is concerned—the love that is the solution to our pride, setting us free from it—you have to "drink" it to know it. By this I mean to has to be received to be known in the deepest sense. This is the idea with which the next chapter begins.

4

THE
NECESSITY
OF
REPENTANCE

Do not confuse Repentance
with Disgust: for the one comes from the Landlord
and the other from the Enemy. . . .

[Repentance] is simply a description of what going back to Him is like.
If you ask God to take you back without it, you are
really asking Him to let you go back without going back. It
cannot happen. (C. S. Lewis, Mere Christianity*)*

*T*HIS SECTION WILL CONTINUE WITH AN EXAMINATION OF WHAT I BELIEVE to be the true nature of repentance. I must devote two chapters to it because of the importance of continual repentance in our daily living, and because of its bearing on holiness.

Old-Fashioned Repentance

I remember sobbing once in an undignified fashion. I had not wept for years. As a child I had been taught not to weep, and the teaching had taken hold. It had been so successful that I had lost a good many of the feelings themselves.

My nose runs when my tears flow, so that I look pretty disgusting. Mucus flows from the end of my chin. Yet on this occasion, such was the despair in my heart that nothing else mattered.

In this chapter I talk about repentance. Here and in the next chapter I also talk about emotion. Nothing I shall say implies either that the essence of our faith is strong emotion or that our worship must be boisterous to be real. Quiet worship can be as profound as enthusiastic celebration.

This is true of repentance as well. Nothing I shall say implies that the essence of repentance is emotion. But since emotion is part of life, both worship and repentance will include an emotional component, especially when we are awakened suddenly to a reality we had successfully suppressed for a long time. In that case, the awakening comes as a shock.

This fact raises an important question: What is the place of emotion in the Christian life? Fanny Crosby writes:

Down in the human heart, crushed by the tempter,

Feelings lie buried that grace can restore;

Touched by a loving heart, wakened by kindness,

Chords that are broken will vibrate once more.[1]

Is she right? I believe she is. I am fast losing my respect for the human sciences of psychology and psychiatry, but it is very clear from their researches that all sorts of feelings exist where we have no access to them. They are buried deep in the human heart, having been "crushed by the tempter." And they are often reawakened when God touches us.

True emotion must be distinguished from *emotionalism*. Emotionalism is the artificial exploitation of people's emotions. When people reacted 250 years ago with genuine emotion to the Holy Spirit, they were accused of "enthusiasm." It was a derogatory term used to describe the behavior of people involved in the renewals and revivals of the time. Fear of enthusiasm was inculcated by the opponents of the renewals.

My Own Awakening

It is no different now. Many of us, particularly from German, British and Scandinavian backgrounds, have repressed emotions. We bury emotions, and they eventually become too painful to face. Having buried them, we no longer realize we have them.

When I was overwhelmed with tears, I had no idea what was buried inside me. As for visions, I have never tried to have them. God alone knows why I do. They come without any warning and at inconvenient times.

Three of us were praying together one Sunday evening many years ago when I was in my late forties (I am now in my seventies). My two companions were kneeling, in true evangelical style, against the seats of chairs in our living room. I didn't have a chair, so I knelt facing the fireplace, but some distance from it. As is often the case when I pray, my eyes were open. As we began to pray, I found myself staring at hands that reached down to me—hands and white-sleeved forearms. It was not a picture in my mind, but something solid, three-dimensional and in full color, hanging, as it were, in space in front of me.

I was aware of several things. First, I was seeing the nail-pierced hands of Christ. They seemed to be suspended between the fireplace and me, four feet in front of me and two feet above eye level. My eyes, as I said, were open. I got the feeling that the suspended arms had been there all my life, only I had not noticed them before. This sounds weird, I know, but it is the only way I can explain what I experienced. I knew instantly that I was not seeing the actual hands of Christ, but God was projecting something from my own brain before my eyes.

The vision was incredibly beautiful, yet terrifying and damning. I experienced dread. My muscles became water. Strength drained out of me. I was a psychiatrist, and in the psychiatric scheme of things visionary experiences are considered hallucinations. But God was waking me up. I did not consider myself an emotional person—but when God draws near, you find things about yourself that you never knew before.

Somehow, all the power and grace of God lay in what I saw. It was an invitation to take hold of Christ's hands. I knew it, and longed to seize them, yet I could not move. My arms hung paralyzed at my sides. I could no more get movement out of them than I could fly. Had you asked me beforehand whether I would like to experience Christ's love, I would have answered, "Of course I would!" Yet when I was faced with an offer of that same love, my bluff was called. Though I did not know it, I was at that time both controlled and controlling, too controlled to respond to passionate love.

Years before, when I was in my early twenties, God had taught me that I feared the experience of his love and was refusing it even though I was a Christian. Now in my early forties he was saying the same thing, this time far more powerfully. I longed with all my heart to grab his hands, to hold them against my face, tears, mucus and all. Yet I could not. I cried out bitterly, begging him to break the psychological walls around me, walls that I hid behind.

One of the men with me said something to the effect that such drastic measures would not be necessary. But I continued to grieve. Newly awakened to what I had been rejecting, and to the grief of the One who offered it, I could not stop. I knew my attitude insulted Christ and my will was still stuck in resistance to, of all things, his love.

Yet I was utterly unable to change. I could only weep in bitter frustration. And still Christ's hands were extended to me. Bitterly, just as Augustine wept before becoming a Christian, I wept—a broken and rebellious Christian. Until that moment I did not know what a proud and rebellious Christian I was.

Biblical repentance is often associated with alarm and weeping. Over their failure to keep the law of Moses about marriage, Ezra (on behalf of the Israelites) and the Israelites themselves wept bitterly: "While Ezra was praying and confessing, weeping and throwing himself down before the house of God, a large crowd of Israelites—men, women and children—gathered around him. They too wept bitterly" (Ezra 10:1).

In Nehemiah 8, as the people realized how far they had departed from the divine covenant, they wept. You weep when your eyes are opened to the wrong you have been doing. "Then Nehemiah the governor, Ezra the priest and scribe, and the Levites who were instructing the people said to them all, 'This day is sacred to the LORD your God. Do not mourn or weep.' For all the people had been weeping as they listened to the words of the Law" (Neh 8:9).

They did not weep because Jews, like most Mediterranean people, are "emotional." There are normal ways and forms of emotional expression. Health consists in part in the normalization of emotional expression. To be newly awakened to something buried in your psyche can be a shattering experience.

Remorse and Repentance

When Peter realized with dismay that he had three times denied his Lord, he wept—also bitterly. "The Lord turned and looked straight at Peter. Then Peter remembered the word the Lord had spoken to him: 'Before the rooster crows today, you will disown me three times.' And he went outside and wept bitterly" (Lk 22:61-62).

Peter's reaction dramatically demonstrates the difference between remorse and repentance. Peter repented. Judas experienced remorse, but no repentance.

Repentance is interpersonal, involving an experience of the pain I have caused someone else, and profound regret for having caused it. The sin that I knew to be wrong now appears far worse. Or, having assumed that my life is my own, I discover that, on the contrary, I have been robbing God of something that is rightfully his. I have robbed God! I have turned my back on him, stealing the life that he created,and using it for my own purposes. What sin could be greater?

Remorse, on the other hand, concerns the individual alone. It reflects personal humiliation, bitterness and self-hatred. For Judas, death was preferable to the picture of himself he had on discovering his terrible error.

> When Judas, who had betrayed him, saw that Jesus was condemned, he was seized with remorse and returned the thirty silver coins to the chief priests and the elders. "I have sinned," he said, "for I have betrayed innocent blood."
>
> "What is that to us?" they replied. "That's your responsibility."
>
> So Judas threw the money into the temple and left. Then he went away and hanged himself. (Mt 27:3-5)

The King James Version tells us that Judas *repented.* Most modern versions use the term *remorse,* even though the RSV and the NRSV stick with *repentance.* And it has to be admitted that the Koine Greek word *metanoia* should be translated "repentance," if you must always translate the same Greek word with the same English word.

In New Testament Greek no word for remorse exists. The language that became New Testament Greek was a commercial language, a lingua franca of the Roman world. Fine distinctions cannot easily be expressed in it. But is the difference between remorse and repentance so subtle? Not really. Morally and behaviorally there is a vast difference between them. In the New Testament you have to judge by the context which word to use. The majority of modern translations correctly translate the word "remorse" in Matthew 27, since Judas was plainly not even thinking about anyone but himself. True, he mentioned Jesus. But he was absorbed with his own self-image. He hated himself with sick self-hatred, loathed what he had suddenly seen himself to be. He preferred death to the sight of his own image.

Repentance, on the other hand, is far removed from self-hatred. The floods of its weeping are formed by tears of wonder at the Savior's love. Modern evangelism seems not to allow adequately for repentance. How often do we see bitter weeping in evangelistic campaigns (except perhaps for a tear here and there)?

Yet tears alone do not constitute repentance. I have seen persons weep bitterly with self-pity *without repenting*. Repentance happens inside you to produce changed behavior. It is an inner change that produces outer changes, whether we weep or not.

Esau experienced remorse, but not repentance. He realized that he had despised his birthright—God's gift to him. His offense was against God.

See that no one is sexually immoral, or is godless like Esau, who for a single meal sold his inheritance rights as the oldest son. Afterward, as you know, when he wanted to inherit this blessing, he was rejected. He could bring about no change of mind [KJV *repentance*], though he sought the blessing with tears. (Heb 12:16-17)

The classic contemporary account of the repentance that initiates an approach to regeneration is found in Charles Colson's *Born Again,* and I will quote extensively from it.[2]

Seeing Oneself for the First Time

On the night of August 12, 1973, we find Charles Colson sitting in his car in the dark. Colson has left politics for law. He had been a marine and then a nothing-is-impossible, ruthless political fighter. He little dreams there is a prison sentence in his future for his alleged association with the Watergate break-in.

Colson has just spent time with Tom Phillips, president of Raytheon Company, the largest employer in New England, and one of Colson's clients. Phillips has recounted the story of a revolution in his life and has read him a chapter from C. S. Lewis's *Mere Christianity.* As heat passed through his body, conviction overwhelmed Colson. Scenes from his earlier life appeared vividly before him, accusing him of the sin of pride. Nevertheless, he courteously refused his host's invitation to stay longer. Pride builds a shell around you.

Tom finished the chapter on pride and shut the book. I mumbled something noncommittal to the effect that "I'll look forward to reading that." But Lewis's torpedo had hit me amidships. . . . *That one chapter had ripped through the protective armor in which I had unknowingly encased myself for forty-two years.* . . . In those brief moments while Tom read, I saw myself as I never had before. And the picture was ugly.[3]

Was there a fear of looking weak in Phillips's eyes? There probably was. We all encase ourselves unknowingly in protective armor. Colson had always prided himself on toughness. Toughness to the point of ignoring other people's finer feelings had gotten him to the top of the political ladder. He tried to explain: "You see . . . I saw men turn to God in the Marine Corps; I did once myself. Then afterwards it's all forgotten and everything is back to normal. Foxhole religion is just a way of using God."[4]

So he had left the house, realizing a moment later that he was making a serious mistake. Now he sits in his car in the dark.

As I drove out of Tom's driveway, the tears were flowing uncontrollably. There were no street lights, no moonlight. The car headlights were flooding illumination before my eyes, but I was crying so hard it was like trying to swim underwater. I pulled to the side of the road not more than a hundred yards from the entrance to Tom's driveway, the tires sinking into soft mounds of pine needles.[5]

Repentance includes release from the impossible burden of running our own lives and from the load of sin of which we may be entirely unconscious. At the very least it comes to us with a sense of relief. And when that burden has been very great, a release of tears accompanies the release. "They weren't tears of sadness or remorse, nor of joy—but somehow tears of relief." But the release is not always accompanied immediately by saving faith.

I had not "accepted" Christ—I still didn't know who He was. My mind told me it was important to find that out first, to be sure that I knew what I was doing, that I meant it and would stay with it. Only, that night, something inside me was urging me to surrender—to what or whom I did not know.[6]

Yet like Paul on the road to Damascus, Colson senses that God is somehow present. "I stayed there in the car, wet-eyed, praying, thinking, for perhaps half an hour, perhaps longer, alone in the quiet of the dark night. Yet for the first time in my life I was not alone at all."[7]

There is also prayer—real prayer, prayer that springs from the heart of a man crying out for God's help: " 'God, I don't know how to find You, but I'm going to try! I'm not much the way I am now, but somehow I want to give myself to You.' I didn't know how to say more, so I repeated over and over the words: *'Take me.' "*

Colson had just experienced true repentance. It happens to Christians and non-Christians alike. It happened to Chuck Colson before he "accepted Christ" and was a sort of doorway through which he later found faith in Christ.

Now the big question: Did Charles Colson *choose* to repent? Was repentance a product of his will?

Who Does the Repenting?

It certainly does not appear that way in Colson's case—or, for that matter, in Paul's, or Augustine's. It looks as though something that Colson had not chosen to do had taken over his life. He had been running away from repentance when he left Tom Phillips's house. Subsequently, however, he had responded as far as he understood. His repeated "Take me, take me" showed his response to what the Holy Spirit was doing in him.

How do we then explain the discrepancy between Peter's command to repent (Acts 2:38) and what occurred in the two incidents I have described?

The teachers in the Brethren assembly where I grew up had no theological training. They were mainly working men—like the apostles. Someone had, however, warned them about legalism. So they warned me to have nothing to do with repentance. They said it carried great dangers of legalism. (I did not then know what "legalism" was, but at the age of eight I nodded wisely.)

Later teachers (fresh from never-mind-which school) insisted that repentance was something you did, not something that happened to you. After all, doesn't the Bible command repentance? Obeying a command means doing something, doesn't it? "The Holy Spirit is the one who brings about the new birth, but you yourself have to repent," my condescending critic pointed out to me. He had recently graduated from seminary and felt my grasp of the truth was shaky. "Repentance," he told me earnestly, "is purely a work of man. It's something you do."

Repentance means to respond to what God is showing you. Your will is involved in response to God's initiative. The time to repent is when the Holy Spirit brings to you not only a true awareness of your sin but also contrition (Is 66:2). Take the case of Peter's sermon on the Day of Pentecost. "You people killed the Messiah!" he told his hearers, in effect (Acts 2:23). Because the Holy Spirit had brought profound conviction to them, they cried out, "Brothers, what shall we do?" (v. 37). The repentance process had begun. It was at that point that Peter told them to repent and be baptized.

You can repent only when the Holy Spirit has brought you conviction. How the two (conviction and repentance, the Spirit's illumination and our response) work together is a divine mystery. The furthest we can go without the Lord's aid is to admit our guilt before God and ask him to let us see it as he sees it.

I am sure that the heat Colson felt indicated the Holy Spirit was falling on him, doing what theologians call *a prevenient work of grace.*[8] As Tom Phillips read Lewis to him, he had seen in horror how God must view his past life. He also saw that his values had been hopelessly wrong. For the first time he was seeing himself as God saw him. For a time, while he was still Phillips's guest, he had resisted what God was trying to do. But by the time he drove away, he was finding resistance extremely difficult. Gradually his defiance of the Spirit broke down, until his tears were truly an acknowledgment of what he had done and a plea for mercy. Examine the way he describes it:

I forgot about machismo, about pretenses, about fears of being weak. And as I did, I began to experience a wonderful feeling of being released. Then came the strange sensation that water was not only running down my cheeks, but surging through my whole body as well, cleansing and cooling as it went.[9]

The Christian life would be very much simpler if we grasped that it consists of working together with whatever the Holy Spirit is seeking to do in and with us. The old aphorism "Let go, and let God!" is not a call to be passive and do nothing. Rather, it is a call to be sensitive to whatever God is doing in our lives, and to collaborate actively with him.

Repentance consists of quitting my resistance to the Holy Spirit, seeing matters God's way and going along with the process. Not repenting is resisting what God is doing, and remaining in rebellion and self-determination. God's Spirit strives patiently with those who resist, but eventually God has to let such people have their own way. His Spirit will not always strive with us.

Esau sinned in selling his birthright and clearly went on resisting the Holy Spirit for years. (See KJV or RSV version of Hebrews 12:16-17.[10]) Finally he was unable to repent, even though he tried to, weeping.

Repentance is rather like conversion. Conversion is turning around and setting off in a new direction. However, the two are not the same. Rather, they overlap. Conversion without repentance is merely reformation. Reformation that does not arise out of repentance is a work of the flesh. It does nothing to the heart of the reformed individual. Nicodemus was a reformed man. So was the rich young ruler. Yet both were in dire need of a change of heart.

We live in a crazy, sin-cursed world. Just moments ago I watched a popular TV program in which the program host, playing God, brought a young paraplegic in a wheelchair and his parents face to face with the former friend who shot him in the neck. The parents and the paraplegic had no intention of forgiving the boy who had done the shooting, and the young aggressor showed no grief about his action. Only accusation and counter-accusation followed: the aggressor accused the victim of fraudulently clinging to his illness and claimed to have seen him take three steps, while the injured man's family accused the aggressor of heartless criminality. Such is the darkness that our world, including the church, is in. Only when our eyes are opened by the Spirit of God himself do we see ourselves and the world as God sees it.

What is it then that makes us Christians? It is that particular form of conversion that results when a sinner enters a relationship with the Savior of sinners. It takes place when the repentant heart trusts Christ for the forgiveness of sin. Having seen myself as I've never seen myself before, I see him too as I've never seen him before. As I trust him, new life is born.

Weeping, Alarm and Repentance

Tears themselves do not represent repentance. True repentance results in a change of behavior. Changed behavior springs from a changed heart. And the term *heart* in Scripture refers not to emotions so much as to the whole person. When *you* change, your behavior changes.

I began by stating that biblical repentance is often accompanied by alarm and weeping. In some people the alarm predominates. Think of the crowd to which Peter preached on the day of Pentecost. Peter had accused them of crucifying God's Messiah. Their terrified response was immediate. Curiously, he did not urge them to believe. After all, their alarm indicated at least their belief in the facts presented. Rather, he called on them to repent of their previous attitude to Christ and, through baptism, to accept Christ's teaching as an evidence of their trust in his messianic mission and divine sonship.

These days I often see weeping along with repentance. I think of a police detective who served on the vice squad of a certain Canadian city but—perhaps illustrating the principle that it "takes a thief to catch a thief"—had himself been guilty of shady behavior, as well as of infidelity to his wife. His second marriage seemed about to fold when Christ found him.

I met him at a conference. Because becoming a Christian was so recent, so fresh in his mind, the emotions of the change were too fresh for him to control. The hard shell behind which his true humanity had been concealed was now destroyed. He had been "a man's man." But in a prayer meeting he sobbed unrestrainedly, not so much with sorrow as with joy and wonder. Falling on his knees, he cried out, amazed afresh by God's love for him and God's grace coming to him: "You have saved and healed[11] me! I don't understand it! How could you . . . ?"

I call this old-fashioned repentance because in many churches it is seen no more. Yet it has begun to occur more frequently—and not because of manipulation by preachers, which is to be abhorred. No platform manipulation can produce divine repentance, for it is a work of God's Holy Spirit. Manipulation is a work of the flesh. But what I call old-fashioned revival is due for a comeback, and I will continue to talk about its true nature in the next chapter.

5

REPENTANCE: FALSE— & TRUE

A true penitent is a sin-loather. If a man loathe that which makes his stomach sick, much more will he loathe that which makes his conscience sick. . . . It is one thing to be a terrified sinner and another to be a repenting sinner. . . . A woman may as well expect to have a child without pangs [labor pains] as one can have repentance without sorrow.

(Thomas Watson, The Doctrine of Repentance)

*T*HOMAS WATSON, THE MAN RESPONSIBLE FOR THE BOOK *THE DOCTRINE OF Repentance* (see the quote above) was a seventeenth-century Puritan theologian. In his exposition of repentance he made it clear that terror, tears, resolutions and reformation are not proofs of repentance. He declared that repentance was a spiritual medicine made up of six special ingredients:

1. Sight of sin
2. Sorrow for sin
3. Confession of sin
4. Shame for sin
5. Hatred for sin
6. Turning from sin

He said, "if any one is left out it loses its virtue."[1] Sorrow is required "because the eye is made both for seeing and weeping. Sin must first be seen before it can be wept for."

Biblical Expressions

Two words for repentance are common, one in the Old Testament—*šûḇ*—and the other in the New—*metanoia.* Both refer to change, changed minds and changed behavior. Yet they do not define repentance so much as describe its effects.

Another Old Testament word that is frequently translated "repentance" is *nāḥam*. This word is also translated "comfort." It comes from the same root as the word used in Isaiah:

Comfort, comfort my people,
 says your God.
Speak tenderly to Jerusalem,
 and proclaim to her
that her hard service has been completed,
 that her sin has been paid for,
that she has received from the LORD's hand double
 for all her sins. (Is 40:1-2)

The forgiveness of our sins, which is part of the process to which repentance leads us, brings comfort. A tender Savior offers forgiveness to us. So I define repentance as a process initiated by the Holy Spirit which brings great comfort to us. Repentance, wrote Charles G. Finney, "involves a change of opinion respecting the nature of sin, and this change of opinion followed by a corresponding change of feeling towards sin."[2]

One change followed by another—a change of *opinion*, followed by a change of *feeling*. The sinner sees himself and the world differently when he repents. "He sees sin, in its tendency, as ruinous to himself and everybody else."[3] And because he sees it differently, he feels differently about it. Things he once longed for he now despises. Others that failed to interest him now take on a new attractiveness. This is what real repentance does, in contrast with pseudorepentance, which is merely reformation.

Since we have already looked carefully at the process whereby Charles Colson began his Christian journey, we may as well see what he has to say about repentance itself:

But the repentance God desires of us is not just contrition over particular sins; it is also a daily attitude, a perspective.

Repentance is the process by which we see ourselves, day by day, as we really are: sinful, needy, dependent people. It is the process by which we see God as he is: awesome, majestic and holy. . . . And [it] so radically alters our perspective that we begin to see the world through God's eyes, not our own. Repentance is the ultimate surrender of the self.[4]

Emotions and Christianity

Our emotions are basically physical things. When we talk about emotion we are really describing what is happening to our bodies. During World War II, I often heard bombs screaming down from an aircraft overhead, followed by loud explosions. When I first heard these sounds, my heart would begin beating hard. Various hormones had begun to circulate in my body. My pulse and blood pressure registered changes. I might say, "What was that?" (I never said, "I feel scared," because I was a young man doing his utmost not to feel scared.)

I gradually became accustomed to the screams of shells and bombs and the rumbling, sometimes ear-splitting roar of nearby explosions. In time I was conscious of no emotional response at all. But now that the war is a thing of the distant past, let a siren scream with a World War II pattern of sound, and my heart throbs sickeningly.

God designed our bodies to respond to danger and to sounds of danger. Our minds interpret the bodily changes as *emotion*.

God made our bodies. He made them with danger-avoiding and danger-preparation responses. We therefore respond to changes in our environment. We refer to our physical responses to change as "emotions," since that is how we experience them.

Scripture is full of emotion. Jonathan Edwards, who spoke of emotions as *affects* and of having them as being *affected*, declared, "Nothing is more manifest *in fact*, that the things of religion take hold of men's souls no further than they *affect* them."[5]

Emotion also arises when things we have buried in our unconscious, usually because we did not want to face them, are suddenly brought into the light. To be sure, the commitments made by many who are powerfully roused and filled with emotion at conferences where the Spirit is poured out will not stand the test of time. But this has to do with the person's response. The gospel seed is good, but the soil may be indifferent. The plant that springs up quickly in shallow soil may, having no root, wither quickly, or it may be sown among the weeds and thorns of worldly cares and thus be choked and strangled (Matthew

13:1-23.) For as Edwards, one of the greatest Christian minds to put pen to paper, declares at the outset of his treatise on religious affections, "TRUE RELIGION, IN GREAT PART, CONSISTS IN HOLY AFFECTIONS."[6]

Edwards devotes long paragraphs to such emotions as fear, hope, love, hatred, desire, joy, sorrow, gratitude, compassion and zeal, citing many scriptural examples of each and declaring, "There never was anything *considerable* brought to pass in the heart or mind of any man living, by the things of religion, that had not his heart *deeply affected* by those things."

So what about the fear that often accompanies the early stages of repentance? Edwards tells us:

> *They tremble at God's word,* they *fear before him, their flesh trembles for fear of him, they are afraid of his judgments, his excellency makes them afraid, and his dread falls upon them,* &c. An Appellation commonly given the saints in Scripture, is, *fearers of God,* or they *that fear the Lord.*[7]

There is little fear of God left in the modern church. As for sorrow, Edwards spends even more time quoting Scripture passages.

> Mat V.4. "Blessed are they that *mourn . . .*" Psa xxxiv. 18. "The Lord is nigh unto them that are of a *broken heart;* and saveth such as be of a *contrite* spirit."[8]

He continues with the theme of Christian emotions for over a hundred pages of tiny double-columned print, distinguishing carefully between false and true emotion (true emotion being an awakening by the Holy Spirit) and pointing to the behavioral changes that follow where the emotions are real. On several pages following, he handles critical correspondence on the theme.

A Gospel Without Repentance

Our day is a day of superficial Christianity. To become a Christian you are supposed to agree to certain correct beliefs. Gradually you learn the Christian jargon and gain confidence in socializing in the Christian community. This is the quick-fix form of Christianity. It tends to produce either reformed sinners or else weak Christians.

Many years ago I was slated to speak at the Massachusetts Institute of Technology. The Christians who had invited me were pessimistic about evangelistic possibilities at MIT. I asked them why. They told me that a year before, a well-known Christian organization had flooded the campus with ardent soul-winners. They made a significant impact on the student body. I forget the figures, but I have the impression that "decisions" numbered more than a thousand.

"How are those Christians doing?" I asked, supposing that since only a year had passed, there would still be lots of enthusiasm.

"Only two remain, as far as we know," my informants replied. "Within a week the converts began to be disillusioned. Whenever we talk about Christ now, they say, 'Yeah, I went through that last year. Forget it, man!' "

Some of the new converts may not have received adequate care, but I am convinced that was not the only explanation. I believe Christ had not been presented adequately. There had been no repentance and no new life in many, perhaps most, of the students.

In our day we do not evangelize. We do a sales job. There is insufficient sensitivity, insufficient spiritual discernment as to where the inquirer is in his or her search. There is almost no preaching for repentance, and most of our preachers have little awareness of God's awesomeness. Quick fix.

Perhaps we will never know how many people who made "decisions for Christ" in the twentieth century actually entered the kingdom of God. Some seem to—their lives bear witness to the fact. But often they struggle, bewildered by promises of Scripture that never seem to work, and by an experience others speak of that eludes them.

If you watch a butterfly as it struggles its way out of its cocoon, you may feel tempted to use a pair of scissors to give it a hand. Sticky strands of "goo" may seem to hold it back. And as its wings begin to unfurl in the sunlight, similar strands seem to impede their full development. Yet the struggles of metamorphosis are necessary. Without the hindrances and the struggles to overcome them, the wings will never develop properly. Your "help" will produce a cripple, incapable of flight.

Christians who have never known repentance are butterflies that have never flown. Not having been through the process that God's Spirit alone initiates, not having resisted, or struggled like Jacob against an invincible antagonist, they have undergone an incomplete process of transition. They are butterflies incapable of flight.

What True Repentance Does

Pain, real pain, is part of the process of repentance. As Chuck Colson sat listening to his friend Tom Phillips, the memories of his past were extremely painful. "Now, sitting there on the dimly lit porch, my self-centered past was washing over me in waves. It was painful. Agony."[9]

This is the pain of facing reality. The story is told of a primitive man who encountered a mirror for the first time. He reacted with horror, disgust and fear to what he saw in it. Apparently he had no idea he was looking at himself. We do not see ourselves as we are, but through one of two mirrors. One belongs to us, and God has another. So we see ourselves either through the mirror of our personal vanity or else—more accurately—through the mirror of divine love. The view through the latter can be shattering. But it can change us forever—if we let it.

That is why great revivals are times of weeping. You will find an account of the first recorded revival in Nehemiah 8. The people of Jerusalem have gathered around one of the city gates to hear a reading from the Law. They had requested the reading. There in the open air, they listen for several hours.

Now, think for a minute. Picture yourself in an open-air meeting with several thousand people. No songs. No loudspeakers. Levites are reading for hours. Under such circumstances, would books like Numbers and Leviticus move you deeply? Yet because the Holy Spirit was active, this is precisely what happened. The crowd wept.

Catholics and Protestants agree about this important truth. Jean LaFrance, a French Jesuit, says, "Discovering your sin is less important than discovering Christ—then you are close to the blessing of tears."[10] He goes on to explain that you "cannot discover [Christ's] face without discovering at the same time what you are rejecting in your heart. This is your real sin."[11]

Weeping is only one of the emotions associated with true repentance. Joy is likely as well—delirious joy over the wonder of sins forgiven, of

God's loving acceptance of me. When the Jews wept in horror over their failure to keep the law, Nehemiah and Ezra ran among them telling them to rejoice. That day was a day for celebration, for God's Word had come to them again! So they rejoiced and had a party (Neh 8:10-12). Tears and laughter are close together when we repent.

A Radical Shift of Attitude

More important than emotion is the profound change in attitude and outlook that repentance brings. It is this that proves the repentance to be genuine. Weeping and laughter can have many causes. False repentance, Charles Finney tells us, "is founded on selfishness."[12]

In many things Finney's theological views differ markedly from my own, but his grasp of the psychology of repentance awes me. For instance, most Christians when testifying or preaching tend to be apologetic about hell and damnation. Those who have experienced true repentance have no such compunctions. Read how Finney describes the person who has truly repented:

> He feels that it would be so right and so reasonable, and so just, for God to condemn him to eternal death, that so far from finding fault with the sentence of the law that condemns him, he thinks it a wonder of heaven . . . that God can forgive him. . . . He is full of adoring wonder that he is not sent to hell.[13]

Again, most of us, when we think we have repented, do not like people to know what God has forgiven us for. Some of our sins, at least, are surely none of other people's business. But the truly repentant person just does not care who knows. "The individual who has exercised true repentance is willing to have it known that he has repented, and willing to have it known that he was a sinner."[14] Finney tells us,

> He who has only false repentance resorts to excuses and lying to cover his sins, and is ashamed of his repentance. . . . Instead of that . . . openhearted . . . frankness, you see a palavering, smooth-tongued, half-hearted mincing out of something that is intended to answer the purpose of a confession, and yet to confess nothing.[15]

One man I know seduced a younger man into a homosexual relationship. He was embittered by the church's response when the matter was discovered. Some years later, however, God brought him into a deep experience of repentance. Eagerly he called the church leaders on the telephone, telling them he wanted to come back to visit the church and do anything he could not only to apologize but to make any possible amends. He was willing, he said, to face any indignation that people might feel. He wanted desperately to make some kind of restitution. He was received warmly into the church and made the profound discovery that shame had left him. So what if everybody knew! God loved him and had blotted his sin out. "True repentance leads to confession and restitution. The thief has not repented while he keeps the money he stole."[16]

There is another very important test of true repentance that distinguishes it from pseudorepentance. It has to do with our attitude to a sin we have truly repented of. True repentance awakens hatred and loathing of a sin you once resisted, but still found alluring. True repentance makes you hate the sin you repented of.

I remember once repenting of masturbating. When the repentance was done, masturbation no longer held me. I did not loathe myself (as I usually had done when I got through masturbating). I hated the sin.[17] I hated the very walls of the room where I had last sinned.

Before that (except for occasional feverish lapses) I had done all in my power not to masturbate. But oh, what allure it could have at times! Absence would make my heart grow fonder of what I later truly loathed!

Finding True Repentance

Sometimes we get a team together to pray for someone with a "besetting sin," looking for some way to get at the root cause. At times this can be appropriate, but often it gets nowhere. We may be dealing with what I call "an inner healing junkie"—someone who is more interested in the wonderful process of hearing other people's powerful prayers than in really becoming a holy person. The real need in that case is for an experience of Holy Ghost repentance.

But how do you repent? If what I have described is the real thing, how do you enter into it?

First, you must truly want to repent. Then you must ask God to search your heart to show you your sins as he sees them. You must call them by their names—even write down a list of them as God searches your heart. Then add to the list your "problems" and ask God whether you should not call them sins rather than problems. Take time in quietness to let God speak. *All the time your focus must not be on your sins but on your Savior, on what your sins cost him and with what love he paid for them.* As far as you are able you must refuse to go on practicing the sins.

You will not entirely succeed in getting rid of the practice of sin. The motions of sin, the attitudes you give way to in your heart, will still plague you. Even if you do succeed, your success will not necessarily represent true repentance. Therefore you must ask God to give you the spirit of true repentance.

It may not come at once, but when you ask God something like that, sooner or later he will answer. By all means go on asking—not that you will be heard for your "many words" (Mt 6:7). What matters is that you keep the matter of repentance in the active file in your own mind. Then one day you will weep. Or maybe the realization of sins forgiven will sweep over you in a way that you have never seen it before, and you will be mad with joy, with "joy unspeakable and full of glory."

Or maybe it will be an altogether more tranquil affair, involving a deep assurance and a new liberation. Whatever the subjective pattern, you will know God has done a deep work within you. Like Chuck Colson, you will know a profound peace. For under the moving of the Spirit of God, you will have repented truly.

Let C. S. Lewis encourage you: "Can we do it if God helps us? Yes, but what do we mean when we talk about God helping us? We mean God putting into us a bit of Himself, so to speak."[18] And when that happens, you will begin to know what experiential religion is all about.

6

TO WORSHIP
A HOLY GOD
IN SPIRIT
& TRUTH

Yet a time is coming and has now come when the true worshipers will worship the Father in spirit and truth, for they are the kind of worshipers the Father seeks. God is spirit, and his worshipers must worship in spirit and in truth. (John 4:23-24)

[Worship] is not a mere act of willpower by which we perform outward acts. Without the engagement of the heart we do not really worship. The engagement of the heart is the coming alive of the feelings and the emotions and affections of the heart. Where feelings for God are dead, worship is dead. (John Piper, Desiring God)

GOD DOES NOT SEEK MERE CONVERTS. HE SEEKS WORSHIPERS. WORSHIP-
ers who worship one God in spirit and truth.

God does not need worshipers, but we need to worship him.
Knowing our need, he seeks to teach us this. True worshipers do not
worship the contemporary gods of money (Mammon) and sex (Baal).
They worship one God alone. All other worship is idolatry.

I was reared understanding what worship was, a fact for which I
shall never cease to be grateful. I soon knew that it embraced the whole
of life—all we do and say. Nothing so elicits my worship and praise as
the thought of God's holiness. The more I become aware of his
kindness, his tenderness, his awesome greatness (all of which are a
part of that same holiness), the more wonder and praise rises from me.

Because of this, I was bewildered by the church that many years ago
invited me to be its minister. The members sang worshipful hymns—sang
them beautifully—but they did not worship. They loved the hymns, loved
them deeply and truly. Yet I could tell by watching their eyes that they
were responding to the hymn itself more than to the God the hymn sought
to praise. It was in their singing that I first noticed the absence of worship.
(Of course, worship is by no means confined to what we sing but should
fill the whole of life and be expressed in all we do.)

After some time the absence of worship began to bother me so much that I decided to invite the elders and deacons to my home, in order to make a real attempt to explain the nature of worship. I talked to them about God's holiness above all. I said that in worship your heart matters much more than your voice, your motive more than what you do or say. I thought my explanation was understood, but I soon found I was mistaken.

On the heels of my little talk I suggested that we worship together. I reasoned that if singing triggered the wrong sort of response, perhaps just expressing our worship in prayer might help. I don't remember exactly what I said, but it was something like "Let's tell God how we feel about his worth. Worship is something we owe him. Why don't we tell him how we see him, express the glory and 'worthship' of his acts and his being?"

What happened next showed me how dismally my explanation had failed. Each in turn prayed, their heads bowed, their voices subdued. One after another they expressed regret for not worshiping and asked God to show them how. But nobody worshiped.

My heart sank. Could they not understand? Or was more than understanding involved? Perhaps if I modeled worship before them, they would *see* what worship was.

So I knelt down and began struggling to express to God his own worth. It was hard. I was totally "out of" worshipful feelings, but I knew God ought to be worshiped, so I struggled on hopelessly. And then it happened.

A rising column of unearthly flame burst through the floor two feet in front of me. It continued to rise, seeming to lick the ceiling before going beyond it. The flames were in the room—at least part of the column was. I was not merely seeing a pretty picture in my head. I was not imagining what I saw. It was far too vivid and alive, far more real than the dimly perceived furniture. I remember the precise color of the flames as they blazed on and on. I was seeing a manifestation of God's holiness, which fire particularly symbolizes in Scripture. God's fire burns both in judgment and in blessing; it is fire that refreshes and renews, and deadly fire that purges destructively.

My worship changed immediately and utterly. My struggles to worship were gone. I was so physically weak that I could hardly stay on my knees. I shook, trembled, wept. My nose began to run, but I didn't care. But oh, how I worshiped! I do not know why God did what he did, except that worship that a moment previously had been hard—almost forced out of me—now flowed from my inner being in floods, hampered only by my sobs and my running nose.

When something happens that puts you in touch either with a frightening memory or with some biblical truth that you had never really grasped with all of your heart, your emotional response is both profound and complex. You are shaken up.

What had I just learned? What was the *intellectual* knowledge that came? I knew, and was appropriately terrified by, a judgment that burns like fire, that consumes dross and human lives that are dross. It comes as judgment as well as quickening. I saw and was shocked, saw and trembled.

It was not the first time I had experienced what some Pentecostals call an open vision. Always when visions have come to me they have been unsought, totally surprising. To seek such experiences would be to expose oneself to danger and deception. Yet when my visionary experiences involve symbol, the symbol is instantaneously comprehensible, as though it is language that my spirit understands automatically. So it was that evening. No "interpretation" of the fire was needed. I was seeing God's holiness, and I knew it.

When a vision of this sort comes, terror overwhelms me, yet never do I love God so much. Always my life is changed thereafter.

I wish I could remember how my visionary experience ended. Did the vision just fade? My memory is blank. I do remember seeing the others with their heads still bowed. Intuitively I knew they did not share my experience. The next thing I recall is shaking each deacon and elder's hand as, one after another, they left the house. Each said roughly the same thing: "Thank you, John. That was very nice."

Nice? I had seen glory. *Nice?*

Emotion and Worship

Let's look again at the second quote at the head of the chapter. John Piper, a biblical scholar, says that worship "is not a mere act of willpower by which we perform outward acts. Without the engagement of the heart we do not really worship. The engagement of the heart is the coming alive of the feelings and the emotions and affections of the heart. *Where feelings for God are dead, worship is dead."*

Is Piper right? Should worship involve "the coming alive of the feelings and the emotions and affections of the heart"? Is it true that "where feelings for God are dead, worship is dead"? Once again the question of our emotions and their place in Christian experience arises.

I must not give the impression that a running nose and sobs are essential to worship. Nor can I suggest that quiet reverence is out. However, I suspect that for many of us "quiet reverence" may cover a meandering mind full of wandering thoughts. The bowed head may conceal absent-mindedness more than reverence. Conversion itself represents becoming alive—waking up to reality. Similarly, sanctification is brought about by a progressive increase of life. An unconscious person has no feelings. The recovery of consciousness is an awakening to a potential range of emotion.

Our feelings fluctuate. At times we are alive to our immediate environment and at others more awakened to spiritual realities. The ideal would be to be aware of both environments at once. Few of us succeed in this. But since sanctification for all of us involves a coming alive of feelings, our feelings will include both the kind we like and the kind we do not like—the jabs of a toothache, the warmth of a fire, the pangs of hunger, the satisfaction of a full stomach. It is when you are dead or even unconscious that you feel nothing. And much of the church is either dead or unconscious.

Sanctification will involve the awakening of feelings that Satan had crushed. Consider once again what Fanny Crosby says. I believe she hits the nail on the head:

Down in the human heart, crushed by the tempter,
Feelings lie buried that grace can restore;
Touched by a loving heart, wakened by kindness,
Chords that are broken will vibrate once more.[1]

With life come feelings—feelings of all kinds, good and bad. God gives life, and with life a wide range of emotional feeling. The suppression of emotion is Spartan—a pagan warrior ideal. It can be accompanied by serious health problems. People of northern European ancestry—

Scandinavians, British and German—have more of such "emotional suppression" problems than Latins. In Germany, John Wimber saw a young German shaking visibly as the power of God's Holy Spirit fell on him. "What are you feeling?" Wimber asked him.

"I not feel *nothing!*" was the heavily accented reply. Yet the man's whole body shook visibly.

Satan, who hates the divine image in human beings, hates its emotional component. Our emotions were meant to reflect God's and to work the way God's emotions work, since this is one of the ways we bear the divine image. God's love for us never gets jaded, his delight in us never fades. Nor should *our* delight in and love for him ever diminish. Rather, they should become fuller, deeper and richer.

This is why Satan likes to rob us of emotions, of our emotional capacities. Where culture places a high value on stoicism and keeping emotions under control, those same emotions are commonly experienced less and less. Not only are expressions of emotion (laughter, weeping, yells of anger) diminished, but even the experience of an emotion is, so that people become less in touch with their emotions. The emotions have been *repressed.* This is one way Satan reduces the image of God in us—through the cultural values we espouse.

Satan seems to take particular delight in robbing us of our pleasurable emotions. He tempts us to pursue them alone. By excessive pursuit of sex and alcohol—sex for its own sake, alcohol for its sensation alone[2]—people discover that the greater the grip of an addiction, the less pleasure it affords. Sexual climaxes get boring; drunkenness becomes a drag. Only when abstinence is instituted for a period does the capacity for pleasure return.

We are dealing with jadedness. Pleasurable emotions indulged as God intended never become jaded. Bodily pleasures are not given for their own sakes but are part of a greater whole. Sexual pleasure is intended to teach us love, to take us beyond ourselves in loving a spouse, in watching the creation of new life and in mirroring the divine unity. Joy in worship is intended to teach us to pursue the source of joy—God himself. Rightly understood, worship never leads to jadedness. On the contrary, it grows deeper and richer.

Fear of emotion, in religion or in any other area of life, is unfortunate.

In one sense there is no limit to emotional experience. Yet clearly there is such a thing as emotional excess. Wherever emotion is pursued *for its own sake,* something has gone profoundly wrong. In worship, especially, we do not pursue emotion: we pursue God.

Most of us are fed up with the conventional Santa Claus and commerce-dominated Christmas. We experience jadedness as the season rolls around each year. But as we turn our thoughts to what God did in the Incarnation and reflect on the wonder of what God has done for us, marvel begins to burn within us. The fire of that wonder can build to incredible heights!

God created our bodies and knows how they function—how we "work," so to speak. He desires to lead us into more and more sharing of his grief and his "joy unspeakable and full of glory." Piper is correct in his view of worship. "Where feelings for God are dead, worship is dead."

Worship and the Power of Sin

Worship is a way of life. Worship must be expressed in our thoughts and in every action. Horatius Bonar sang,

Fill now my life, O Lord my God,
in every part with praise;
that my whole being may proclaim
your being and your ways.
Not for the lip of praise alone,
nor yet the praising heart,
I ask, but for a life made up
of praise in every part.[3]

It begins with the presentation of our bodies to God. The presentation is an act of adoration and worship. Paul writes, "Therefore, I urge you, brothers, in view of God's mercy, to offer your bodies as living sacrifices, holy and pleasing to God—this is your spiritual act of worship" (Rom 12:1).

To give your body to God as a living sacrifice constitutes a "spiritual act of worship," Everything you are and do is done with and in your body. You think with your body, for your brain is part of your body. Anywhere you go, you take your body. You cannot leave it behind. To give your body to God, then, is to give everything you do or think or say—from the most mundane and necessary ablutionary act to the most sublime and glorious activities you engage in. To give your body to God is to give away all you are and have. It belongs to him anyway. But you can see what enormous implications the gift has. Think well before you give God your body.

Either you give your body to God, or you automatically give it to—*somebody else*. In practical terms nobody belongs to themselves. Dark powers retain certain degrees of control in our lives, even though by right our bodies belong to God. It has been said that there is no microsecond in time or cubic micron in space that is not hotly contested by Christ and dark powers. Worship of money, sex or of anything else results in a loss of control to the powers of darkness.

Hence Paul's bewilderment at his own actions: "I know that nothing good lives in me, that is, in my sinful nature. For I have the desire to do what is good, but I cannot carry it out. For what I do is not the good I want to do; no, the evil I do not want to do—this I keep on doing" (Rom 7:18-19). The law of sin that Paul speaks of is in all of us. It is a driving force pushing us into sin, often without our awareness. John Owen says it "invades the soul secretly and makes it gradually insensitive to sin."[4] Only when we fight sin do we become painfully aware of our struggle, as Paul did.

But there is a more sinister side to the problem. Whether we struggle against sin, conscious of its power, or give way to it without any awareness, we must be aware of more than ourselves and our sin. Spiritual beings "goad us into sin."[5] We are tempted, seduced, pushed. They want power over any being who bears God's image. Once we strive to live holy lives we become aware of our helplessness. *For by our unwitting worship we have given false gods power over our lives.* Only Christ can break their control.

Worshipers of One God Only

At the core of any religion you find worship. It is foundational to all religion. False religions teach adherents to worship the powers of darkness as "gods." The gods are worshiped, adored, reverenced.

One of the distinctives of Christian faith is that it deals with sin. It plants our feet on the way of holiness. It should not surprise us, then, to find that worship of the true God is an important key to holiness.

God's claim to be worshiped is an exclusive claim. Moses made it very plain to Israel that there was only one God. He alone had delivered the Israelites from cruel and oppressive slavery. They were to worship only him. Other gods were false.

In other agricultural societies of the ancient Near East the issue was simple. In a ritual sex act with a temple prostitute, you exchanged your bodily seed for the pseudodivinity's promise of multiplied crops and animals. The Israelites had been taught that good harvests come by the grace of Yahweh. But, many of them reasoned, if Israel could secure the benefit of other gods who would throw in exciting religious sex—why not? Thus it was that the miracles of the Sinai, the Red Sea, the divided Jordan were all forgotten.

The following verses are as important today as they were to Israel in ancient times. The New Covenant has done nothing to change the basic realities they point to.

You shall have no other gods before me. (Ex 20:3)

Be careful to do everything I have said to you. Do not invoke the names of other gods; do not let them be heard on your lips. (Ex 23:13)

Do not follow other gods to serve and worship them; do not provoke me to anger with what your hands have made. Then I will not harm you. (Jer 25:6)

I could cite many other verses on the "one God only" theme. And your reaction may be "Of course! We all know there is just one true God. No one I know ever mentions other gods. We bow before no idols."

There was a time when I too could not understand why God would repeatedly insist on this "one God only" theme to me. I was then writing *Eros Redeemed*. Gradually as I examined how both Old Testament and New address the issue of sexual sin, I began to see that by the church's flagrant fall into sexual sin we had come under the power of the ancient sex gods (fallen angelic beings posing as gods). We had made a god of our sexual sensations and had chosen to come under the power of dark beings God had delivered us from. We were not worshiping one God only.

Part of the difficulty lay in an attenuated gospel, with no real proclamation of repentance. We had been processing sinners into the kingdom through mass evangelism, and the result was a passive population of mass-produced converts. Many were psychological converts. There were "tares among the wheat" as well as half-converted people with life but no power—"butterflies without wings," incapable of flight. And like the ancient Israelites, as a church we had come to worship the ancient gods—Baal, Astarte, Moloch, to name only a few.

Again and again as I pondered these things God would speak to me about my devotion to him, insisting that I worship him alone. It grieved me. Did he not understand? Slowly light began to dawn. I noticed that many contemporary Christian songwriters were picking up the same theme of "no other gods." And as I reflected on the most powerful god in the West, Mammon, I realized that the whole society, Christians included, had bowed to this false god.

Mammon's Hold on the Church

You worship whomever you trust. Most of us trust Money more than we trust God. It hit me when God once said to me, "When I ask you to give money to someone and tell you how much to give, *do not consider how much you will have left. I will take care of you!* You are to trust me, not the money you have left in your account!"

That shook me. I had known in the past what it was to trust God alone. I went to the mission field with no promise of support, when the world was still divided into sterling and dollar regions. I had determined not to use prayer letters to hint about my needs. God met me all the way. Not until I began working for the IFES[6] did I know what it was to receive a regular salary.

To receive that salary was to come into a sphere where the kingdom of God was tied to the world economy. *I do not believe that God's kingdom is dependent on this world's economy.* The world's economy is based on human greed. It is an economy of Mammon worshipers, and we, like ancient Israel, have mixed our Christianity with Mammon worship.

You protest. You say, "But you are suggesting a very high standard that God calls few people to follow." I disagree. Salary or no salary, the standard is the same for all of us. We give whenever God tells us to, to whomever or whatever he tells us to give. The standard I struggle for is the norm. It is what we all should practice.

The poor and the oppressed are all around us. I have in my possession the old video *Viva Cristo Rey*, which recounts the remarkable work of God at a dump site between El Paso in the United States and Ciudad Juárez in Mexico. Mexican and American Spanish-speaking families eked out a miserable existence on the dump site.

In the late 1970s, two priests decided to arrange a sort of party for both groups. On the appointed day, the volunteers loaded vehicles full of food and drove to the site. Once there, however, they discovered that they had brought food for 125 people and 360 had turned up. But they prayed over the food and began serving it anyway. To their surprise, everyone who came was served, and there was food left over—I believe five pickup trucks were filled with what remained.

Miraculous? I am inclined to think so. God has not changed. He multiplies resources to those who worship only him. Those who trust him do the best they can with the little they have, giving it all to him.

In Ciudad Juárez and elsewhere, many Christians have learned the importance of reaching out to the poor. Once again the church is facing its responsibility to reach the poor with God's mercy and ours, teaching them the gospel, giving them hope, teaching them to work. It is for the church to solve the welfare problem, and at a local level.

Let me get back to money and me. I was shaken to see that somehow I had slipped into trusting my management of "my" funds, and trusting the funds themselves more than God. This blocked my ability to hear him on the issue of money. Without realizing what I had done, I had been trying to worship two "gods," God and Mammon. Jesus taught us that to do so was impossible: "No one can serve two masters. Either he will hate the one and love the other, or he will be devoted to the one and despise the other. You cannot serve both God and Money" (Mt 6:24).

Is Mammon truly a "god"? I believe so. So does Jacques Ellul. He goes so far as to suggest that we must desecrate Mammon's altar by treating money contemptuously.[7] I haven't quite got there yet! But I am convinced that money is not given us to hoard. Saving might be good for the economy. After all, it is *Mammon's* economy. We are to be channels, not savers, of every divine resource.

Mammon, whoever and whatever he is (and we might as well adopt the name Christ used), is the second most powerful "god" around. Have not the pundits pronounced wise words about Death and Taxes? Satan (lord of death) and Mammon seem to work in one another's pockets. Both crave worship. That is the coin they appreciate.

Thankful Hearts

Anyone who is a true worshiper has a grateful heart—a heart that sings. Holiness, you may remember, while being much more than a feeling, is nevertheless easier "felt than telt." P. T. Forsyth said that holiness "is *realized* by experience, it proceeds in experience; but it does not proceed *from* experience. . . . Our faith is not in our experience, but in our Saviour."[8] But holiness is still felt, still an experience, whatever else it may also be. And it is an experience for which the recipient is extremely grateful, not so much for the holiness itself as for the love and the grace of the God who gave it. As you receive both imparted righteousness and holiness, they became all of a piece once again. You are equally grateful for both, just as for all God's kindness. Gratitude and worship flow almost uninterrupted from your heart.

That is not to say that you live free from pain or distress. Suffering is part of our earthly lot. In fact your capacity for pain grows in proportion to your capacity for joyful adoration. But joy and thankfulness triumph when we worship one God alone. Just as in good music a minor key blends with the major, so the joy and suffering, equally part of Christian experience, blend together. But—and I insist on it—the joy and gratitude win out. The minor never overwhelms the major.

When martyrs sing on the way to their deaths, we must not suppose that they are merely being brave and heroic. That many of them sing cannot be denied. That many appear joyful and triumphant is equally clear. But we are seeing *true joy,* not a heroic effort to portray it. What we see is a reflection of the wonder, the glory they are experiencing as they suffer. They have glimpsed heaven, as Steven did at his trial: "But Stephen, full of the Holy Spirit, looked up to heaven and saw the glory of God, and Jesus standing at the right hand of God. 'Look,' he said, 'I see heaven open and the Son of Man standing at the right hand of God' " (Acts 7:55-56).

I know, even from those visions of glory that have come to me, that one can be caught up into a something, a somewhere, where one discovers the glory that lies beyond, and the Savior who rewards us with it. In such circumstances it is not merely easy to praise, but impossible not to.

It is so as we grow in holiness. To follow the path of progressive holiness is not a matter of passing examinations by dint of great effort, but of discovering the kindness of a God who shares his holy nature freely with us. He wants us to be like himself, so that he can have pleasure with us. He says, "You are to be holy to me because I, the LORD, am holy, and I have set you apart from the nations to be my own" (Lev 20:26).

The Father longs for his children. The Son longs for his bride. The Spirit longs to please both Father and Son, and to present us to both. Pain there will be here and now, but it will be pain overwhelmed by unspeakable joy and glory. I weep for joy more frequently than for pain.

A Life Transformed

Earlier I said that giving your body in worship "is to give everything you do or think or say—from the most mundane and necessary ablutionary act to the most sublime and glorious activities you engage in." Worship makes the commonplace a source of wonder, touches loveliness with a heavenly glory and makes pain a doorway to adoration.

Our lives are made up of the ordinary. Do you worship while you brush your teeth? It's not a duty—heaven forbid! Christian legalism is feeling that you *have* to worship while you clean your teeth! But someday it may strike you that to have teeth at all is an incredible blessing. Many elderly people in developing countries have few or none. Dentures are beyond them. They manage as best they can. To have teeth, and to be able to clean them, is a wonderful gift.

I mentioned the unmentionable—ablutions, a polite term for those things we do in a bathroom. Family life tends to force you to be more tolerant of such things, but once the children grow up we slip back into our need for privacy and shame. Satan has taught us that certain of our physiological functions are shameful. We discover how shameful when we have to "perform" in the presence of other human beings. I hate bedpans! I hate communal bathrooms! My dignity is protected by walls. But secrecy and shame go together.

I have fallen for Satan's line, that defecation and urination are shameful. I try desperately hard not to make noises. And if some full-of-flatus saint makes a noise, we all pretend it hasn't happened.

"Fill thou my life, O Lord my God, *in every part with praise?*" In every part? In ablutions? In defecating and urinating? I believe so. Many older men face difficulties passing urine. Many women who have borne children face difficulties retaining it. When I see men, women and children in Rwanda lying in the products of their dysentery because they are too weak to move, I am profoundly thankful that I have a clean bathroom to go to and medical services to help me. I am grateful for reasonable health and for the marvelous mechanisms that God has created within me to govern my physiology. Slowly I begin to see the marvel of my own creation, and to worship the God who created even these parts of me.

7

MYSTERIOUS WIND

The wind blows wherever it pleases. You hear its sound,
but you cannot tell where it comes from
or where it is going. So it is with everyone born
of the Spirit. (John 3:8)

I ONCE FELT I HAD THE DOCTRINES OF THE HOLY SPIRIT IN MY BACK POCKET. I had them "taped."

I no longer feel this way. The more I know of God's ways, the more I know "I don't know nothin'." The mystery of godliness is great. The same Spirit who awoke me to sin's peril is the Spirit who imparts righteousness to me and the Spirit who sanctifies me. But he is also the Spirit who empowers me—and it is easy to get confused at this point.[1]

The Scandal

Power is imparted by grace. God sovereignly gives power to whomever he wishes. I know that his wisdom is far greater than ours and that God knows what he is doing. *All power belongs to God, who as Creator and Sustainer of the universe is the only source of power.* Satan absconded, as it were, with the power God had given him. God's callings and gifts are "irrevocable" (Rom 11:29), and people who have received power from him can use those powers to gratify their own ego—that is, use them in the service of Satan.

I confess that it bothers me to see God giving power to people who cannot apparently handle it. However, I see this in Scripture as well as in the church today.[2] Samson had great power. His natural strength was greatly enhanced by the Holy Spirit, yet he used the Spirit's power inappropriately—such as when he used it to gain the favor of a prostitute. At that time God wished to deal with the Philistines, showing them who was God. His purposes were broader and more comprehensive than Samson's life.

How do we know that the power came from God and not the devil? How do we ever know? We know in two ways.

First, we know as we understand the purposes of God on this earth. He desires that his name, or character and nature, be made widely known in the earth. He desires people to know that his holiness includes his kindness and sovereign grace in saving and healing men and women. In 1906, when the Pentecostal movement began to spring up in North America, its power was attributed to the devil. But we can know that the miraculous power accompanying the early days of the movement was of God. How? By the vast gospel outreach that resulted, and the many churches that were formed to meet the needs of so many converts—particularly among the poor.

Second, we can know it is God's power by its immediate results in the empowered person. Close contact with God has effects. Where the encounter is genuine, they include a greatly increased love for God, a correspondingly great love for other people—sinners and saved—a love of Scripture and of prayer, increased ability to hear the voice of the Holy Spirit, and an evangelistic impulse.

But these effects are temporary. The "sanctification" will not last.

The Two Operations of the Spirit

Newspapers, magazines and television in Canada, the United States, Britain and Europe have given considerable publicity to the work of the Holy Spirit in the Airport Vineyard in Toronto in the mid-1990s. Several thousand churches in Britain, many of them Anglican, and others in Europe, Australasia, Africa and Singapore have been affected by a related wave of renewal. Guy Chevreau, writing about events in the Airport Vineyard, reports that a steady stream of "over 4,000 pastors and leaders from Britain, Chile, Argentina, Switzerland, France, Germany, Scandinavia, South Africa, Nigeria, Kenya, Japan, New Zealand and Australia have come to receive the outpouring."[3] The publicity surrounding the renewal has brought before us questions regarding how the Holy Spirit works and how we are to think about the strange phenomena that sometimes accompany revivals.

There are two broad ways in which the Spirit works. God awakens, converts, saves and sanctifies: that is one operation. He empowers: *that* is a different operation. This book is about the sanctifying process. But because some people, particularly those in the holiness tradition, believe that the baptisms or anointings of the Spirit are the highway to sanctification, I want to present an alternative point of view. Because the two operations of the Spirit are different, and because the Spirit's power is more necessary today than it has ever been, I devote this chapter to the differences and similarities between the two.

In the traditional holiness view, holiness ("entire sanctification") arose from a second work of grace. You had an instantaneous experience by which the Holy Spirit conveyed holiness. Proponents of this view claimed validation from John Wesley's teaching in his little book *A Plain Account of Christian Perfection*. The doctrine had its true beginning, however, with George Fox (1624-1691), who founded the extreme left wing of the Puritan movement in the mid-seventeenth century. It was called the Society of Friends and has come to be known as "the Quakers" from the fact that when the Holy Spirit fell on people they would shake. Fox was frequently imprisoned, but his force of character and speech won many to Christianity. Today many conservatives still react with suspicion to Fox, but the experience of the Spirit that he had was real. *It just did not have to do with sanctification.*

In his own day, Martyn Lloyd-Jones revived the underlying issue by his very life. This British pastor was a conservative evangelical, yet no one questions the spiritual power that he displayed in ministry. He himself understood what it was, because he was well versed in the long history of the outpourings of God's Spirit. Where did Lloyd-Jones's power come from? Leigh Powell knew, and made the following observation: "At times, often toward the end of the sermon, he seemed to be hovering, waiting for something. . . . Sometimes the wind of the Spirit would come and sweep us and him aloft and we would mount with wings like eagles into the awesome and felt presence of God."[4]

I would like to say that the Spirit's two operations are utterly separate, but this is not really so. There seem to be *sanctifying "spinoffs" from the Spirit's empowering work, and power "spinoffs" from his sanctifying work.* We cannot have any experience of the Holy Spirit's power without something of God's character imparting itself to us. In the wake of renewal you feel like praying more, reading Scripture more, sharing your testimony with others, and you do all this and more. Unhappily, the feelings do not endure. Sooner or later they pass.

Yet the feelings were not the result of false enthusiasm, but of God's Spirit. Faith means trusting that the God who first revealed truth to me will not abandon me. So it is that though feelings may play a part in awakening our slumbering spirits, faith and constancy must be developed. Faith endures to the end.

The temporary nature of our feeling states becomes particularly striking when people are "drunk in the Spirit." I think of Steve, a pastor I know well. After his second visit to the Airport Vineyard (he had been skeptical after his first visit), for four days he was drunk on the Spirit of God. That is, he was unsteady on his feet, his speech was slurred, and he fell on the floor frequently, sometimes passing out entirely. In addition he was emotionally labile. He would weep inconsolably (rather like a maudlin drunk) or laugh uproariously. When he tried to talk sensibly, he would forget what he was saying and get thoroughly confused, sometimes wandering hopelessly from his original point. It would bother him, for he would be half-aware of what he was doing. Of what use was his strange condition? What purpose did it serve?

I was constantly in touch with Steve by telephone during this time, and I flew out to see him on the afternoon of the fourth day. That evening, I remember, he attempted to lead a church meeting. It was a mighty struggle. He tried to explain to the congregation what was happening, but got very muddled in the attempt. He frowned with concentration while members of the congregation grinned and nudged one another. They liked him, and they understood what was happening.

The next day Steve's drunkenness ended. From that point on he was filled with far greater power of the Spirit than he had ever been.

Empowering and Sanctification

Some Christians have no use for instantaneous visitations of the Holy

Spirit, even suggesting that they are from the pit. This is very sad. Some of the sanctifying effects of a "close encounter" with the Holy Spirit may not last; but we still need power.[5] And we cannot expect much power without the Holy Spirit's repeated "falling" on us.

Lloyd-Jones says, "If your doctrine of the Holy Spirit does not include this idea of the Holy Spirit falling on people, it is seriously, grievously defective."[6] He was not referring specifically to spiritual drunkenness here, but the series of sermons that gave rise to his book *Joy Unspeakable* make it clear that Lloyd-Jones had strong and positive feelings about what he termed "baptism with the Spirit." He had clearly experienced such a baptism, and strongly recommended that others seek it.[7] According to Lloyd-Jones, "It is possible for us to be believers in the Lord Jesus Christ without having received the baptism of the Holy Spirit."

Unusual phenomena are often associated with such baptisms (or anointings). Some people become altogether too fascinated by drunkenness or other phenomena associated with the Spirit's falling; Lloyd-Jones urged them—and us—"Do not start thinking about phenomena."[8]

When the Holy Spirit comes on you, falls on you, rests on you or fills you, you receive a refreshing, an empowering to a greater or lesser degree. The empowering may or may not come with what I referred to as "sanctifying spinoffs."

Take my pastor friend Steve. On the fifth day he was no longer drunk. He told me, "Ever since this started, the sense of the Lord's presence has been so real! I fall asleep worshiping him, and my first thought on waking is to praise him and love him." His love for people around him, for the Scripture and for prayer were greatly enhanced in the wake of his experience with the Spirit.

And the power of God filled him. His sermons caused people to weep. Once I watched as he prayed for a Pentecostal pastor-friend who visited a service at Steve's church. As Steve touched him lightly, the Pentecostal pastor fell to the ground like a sack of potatoes. He stayed there unconscious for some time, and needed assistance when the time came for him to leave.

I have heard of people pushing others over in renewal services. I'm sure the report is true. It is amazing how far some preachers will go to maintain their reputation. But Steve did not push. And his friend appeared drunk as he left the building, just as Steve himself had been. Power was present in Steve, a level of power that had not been present before my friend had his experience of the Spirit falling on him.

Judge what happened to Steve by the results in his life, which were wholly good. Nevertheless, these effects in themselves were not true holiness. It is here that I believe the holiness movement missed the point.

I agree with Lloyd-Jones that we must not begin by focusing on the phenomena of the Holy Spirit. Some Christians, especially Pentecostals, have focused almost exclusively on tongues. Today many people are enthralled with other manifestations.

I travel much. Ever since the international exposure[9] of the Airport Vineyard in Toronto, I have noted the lack of sanctifying graces in some who (admittedly a minority) came to Toronto to be empowered, found themselves on the floor and, thinking of this as the "ultimate experience," returned home proud, despising lesser mortals who had not been to Toronto. Such people tend to think "hitting the floor" or manifesting some other sign of the Spirit is everything. It isn't. As Eleanor Mumford put it, "It's not how you go down that matters, *but how you come up!*"[10] Most people come up charged with new love, new zeal. But apart from a bit of spinoff, "hitting the floor" (or whatever else may happen as a sign of the Spirit's empowering) does not sanctify.

Let me get back to my pastor friend, Steve. I next met him about six months later, again in Toronto, but this time at a "Catch the Fire" conference put on by the Airport Vineyard in the Constellation Hotel. On the last morning I found Steve on the front row. How was he?

He was an unsanctified mess. For the previous three months he had been depressed and quite grouchy. There were good reasons for the grouchiness, but the first thing to note is that depression and grouchiness are not hallmarks of sanctification. He was far, far removed from the wonder and the glory he had experienced six months before.

I repeat: *Anointings of the Holy Spirit may have temporary sanctifying spinoffs. But they do not sanctify.*

During the "ministry period" (when people prayed for one another),

I said to Steve, "Look, I'm coming home with you. I'll stay overnight. You need help." He grabbed me and clung to me, sobbing. At his home the Lord enabled me to help. His joy and all that went with it (desire for the Word and prayer, evangelistic zeal) were fully restored.

What Scripture Teaches Us

Throughout the Old Testament the Spirit of God would rest on or be poured on certain people, enabling them to do what they could not have done in their own strength. We are not only indwelt and made alive by the Holy Spirit, but are equipped by him to work in his kingdom and to conquer the dark powers as soldiers of Christ. In general the Bible uses the preposition *on* or *upon* to describe the operation by which he imparts this enabling to us. And the references to his enabling exceed in number even those that have to do with his indwelling. The Spirit rests on or upon people (Is 11:2); he is shed on or upon; he comes on, is poured on, is poured out on or upon them (1 Sam 10:10; 19:20, 23; Is 32:15; Ezek 39:29; Joel 2:28-29; Zech 12:10). There are examples of this in the New Testament as well (Acts 2:33; 10:44).

Various figures of speech are used to refer to this event. For instance, 2 Kings 3 says "the hand of the LORD" (God's power) rested on Elisha, enabling him to predict the future.

Elisha said to the king of Israel, "What do we have to do with each other? Go to the prophets of your father and the prophets of your mother."

"No," the king of Israel answered, "because it was the LORD who called us three kings together to hand us over to Moab."

Elisha said, "As surely as the LORD Almighty lives, whom I serve, if I did not have respect for the presence of Jehoshaphat king of Judah, I would not look at you or even notice you. But now bring me a harpist."

While the harpist was playing, the hand of the LORD came upon Elisha . . . (vv. 13-15)

The hand of the Lord came on Elisha when a harpist played contemporary psalm music. It came to enable him to do something that no prophet can do without the Spirit's aid. When, and only when, that hand was present could Elisha predict the future.

The New Testament speaks of the same phenomenon of empowering, but the language changes somewhat. The expressions here have to do with baptism with the Spirit and being filled with the Spirit. It was as a result of being filled with the Spirit that some of the apostles appeared drunk at Pentecost (Acts 2:1-13). A person who begins to speak a recognized language fluently would not for that reason be accused of drunkenness; thus it appears that something besides speaking in tongues was going on at the same time. I am convinced that it was this phenomenon that led Paul to write, "Do not get drunk on wine, which leads to debauchery. Instead, be filled with the Spirit" (Eph 5:18). For I have seen a good deal of that same "drunkenness" recently. It must be judged by its results, which are (1) empowering and refreshing in the work of the kingdom plus (2) temporary holy feelings.

Total Sanctification?

I know that some believers talk about total sanctification, referring to an operation of the Holy Spirit by which sin is totally eradicated in us, but this is not my own understanding of what happens. John Wesley wrote about a perfecting of love in us, but he was not describing a total perfection. In any case, one can be deceived by experiences that do not have an underlying biblical foundation.

As I write, powerful renewal is taking place in churches of all types around the globe. People collapse on the floor, even being flung down. Some laugh, others weep and sob. There can be shaking and agonized outcries. I have mentioned already that I described such manifestations in *When the Spirit Comes in Power.*

However, some leaders see the outpouring as the key to everything—see it, in fact, as a key to the character change of holiness. And certainly it has sanctifying aspects. It causes some people, for example, to be deeply conscious of Christ's presence in their lives. Martyn Lloyd-Jones acknowledges a connection between such experiences and sanctification, but cautions: "But we must be careful here. Though that is what one feels at that point, it does not mean that sin has been entirely eradicated. That is what one feels at the time, but it is not so."[11] He goes on to say, "There is always this connection between baptisms with the Holy Spirit and sanctification. . . . [But] if we do not find obvious evidence of sanctification in those who are claiming great experiences or great gifts, we must warn them solemnly in the name of God, show the danger to them."[12]

Nevertheless, he warns of a far greater danger. "What do we know about these great manifestations of the Holy Spirit? We need to be very careful 'lest we be found fighting against God,' lest we be guilty of quenching the Spirit of God."[13] Again he warns, and the warning appears repeatedly in the same book, written in the mid-twentieth century:

And if your doctrine of the Holy Spirit does not include this idea of the Holy Spirit falling on people, it is seriously, grievously defective. This, it seems to me, has been the trouble especially during this present century, indeed almost for a hundred years. The whole notion of the Holy Spirit falling on people has been discountenanced and discouraged, and if you read many books on the Holy Spirit you will find it is not mentioned at all, a fact which is surely one of the prime explanations of the present state of the Christian church.[14]

Creation Renewed

The point Paul makes in the last part of 2 Corinthians 3 is that God's work of imparting glory to the Christian is not merely to be passive and progressive, but (excuse the alliteration) *permanent*. At least, this is what God intends it to be. It is forever.

And it is a glory that will subsequently be revealed to the whole creation. In Romans 8:18-25 Paul writes about the day when that glory will finally be made clear in all of us. If we want to understand the future prepared for us, there is no more important passage anywhere in Scripture.

Paul says that the earth groans. Some of us groan along with the earth, and for the same reason. In fact the whole creation "has been groaning as in the pains of childbirth" (v. 22), longing for the freedom it once enjoyed. As I walk through the woods near my home (and British Columbia woods are very beautiful), I see the endless struggle between life and death, and groan as I see it. I see the beauty of new life. But the rotting trees reveal the horror of death and decay. Death never wins an absolute victory, and life has always triumphed; still, the universe groans from the bondage of that curse God placed on it at the beginning of time, when Satan's terrible reign began.

What is creation's hope? To be set free from that curse. The curse began, and the reign of death with it, when humankind listened to and obeyed the voice of darkness. It will be set free "from its bondage to decay and brought into the glorious freedom of the children of God" (v. 21) when the glory of those who bear the image of God bursts onto the scene. Read the whole passage.

I cannot tell you how great the joy this passage gives me. Because I feel the burden of creation's bondage, I can anticipate the wonder of what is to come. All creation waits for a marvelous day in the future when certain beings known as "the children of God" will be shown to be what they truly are. John 1:10-13 clarifies that these are persons "born not of natural descent, nor of human decision or a husband's will, but born of God." We ourselves are part of that line. Down history's ages there have always been sons and daughters of the living God, and the creation groans with longing for their revelation. It will be a revelation of glory.

Creation groans in childbirth as I write. It is going to be set free when the divine offspring of God are shown in their true colors. In that day the end result of the passive, progressive *and* permanent transformation will be absolutely clear.

The Lesson I Learned in La Paz

The airport in La Paz, Bolivia, must be more than fourteen thousand feet above sea level. It lies in the *altiplano*, a high plateau, close to the famous Lake Titicaca, where balsam boats are still in use, and overlooked by the everlasting snows of the "sacred" mountain of Illimani.

Years ago when my wife Lorrie and I were rookie missionaries, a kind Quaker couple met our flight when we landed at La Paz. We had rarely encountered anyone so kind and good. Their faces were radiant with joy and peace.

At the baggage claim I picked up our heavy suitcases and began to carry them, but suddenly I grew dizzy and began to sway. The Quaker husband seized my suitcases saying, "Here, let me take them—or you'll be getting *serroche!*" He made me sit down for a few moments. *Serroche* is a Bolivian expression meaning altitude sickness. Our sudden ascent to an unaccustomed altitude, coupled with my struggle with two heavy bags, had left me lacking in oxygen.

The Quakers invited us to their home, and we descended along the winding road down into La Paz. We sat in their lounge as they served us tea, and they began to describe to us a recent "sanctifying experience" that had filled them with "joy unspeakable." It had affected both of them equally, and I have no doubt about the genuine nature of the experience. It certainly was of God.

Had they been living among Quakers of like mind, they might never have discovered that the love and joy they had experienced (to say nothing of their newfound joy in testifying to saved and unsaved) was a refreshing and empowering experience and that its "sanctifying effects" could be temporary. But they were not surrounded by like-minded Quakers who shared their views. They were in the midst of pagan strongholds in one of the "high places" of the earth. The powers of darkness ruled in their immediate proximity. Had I known then what I know now, I would have warned them. But I was even greener than they, and I merely listened with a yearning heart to the experiences they shared.

Six months later I learned that the kind, warmhearted Quaker man had gone off to Lima to live with a Peruvian woman to whom he had felt an adulterous attraction.

Had I been utterly mistaken in his character? Not at all. Rather, I had been ignorant of the very dangers I am talking about: the dangers of confusing the two operations of the Spirit of God. I had also had only a superficial grasp of the deadly power of hell in the "high places" of the earth.

Many in the Reformed tradition know much about sanctifying doctrines, but little of the Holy Spirit's refreshing and empowering. Many in the holiness tradition know a good deal about the Spirit's empowering, but not enough about sanctification. As the end times approach, it becomes increasingly important that we know and benefit from both operations.

The Law of Sin

Our problem is inherited sinfulness. We have a vulnerability, a proclivity to commit sin which frustrates us as much as it frustrated Paul. "I do not understand what I do. For what I want to do I do not do, but what I hate I do," he writes in Romans 7:15.

Some of us struggle with a bad temper. We bite our lips and do our utmost to control it. Mostly it works. But sooner or later we get caught out, and *boom!*—we explode. And then we mentally curse ourselves. Just lose a couple of nights' sleep and see what that does to your temper! Wait till you get cerebral arteriosclerosis and see what it does to your self-control! For self-control, fruit of the Spirit, does not mean control by me, *but control of me by the Holy Spirit.* He, not I, must be in control.

Some of us have no difficulty with our tempers but struggle with something else. For the Quaker missionary in La Paz it was a vulnerability to sexual sin. From thinking himself perfectly sanctified to succumbing to adulterous sex was a much shorter step than he supposed.

Holy feelings are not holiness. We can have real experiences of sensing God's presence and closeness, but these are neither sanctification nor sanctifying experiences. Not to be aware of the two operations of the Holy Spirit is dangerous. Many people well schooled in Reformed doctrine need to be told that *having a grasp of the doctrines of sanctification does not sanctify,* while people with holiness backgrounds need to understand that the Spirit's falling on a person *will not produce holiness.*

Reformed folk should get back to the doctrines of the Reformers, especially the later Welsh Puritans, who understood outpourings of the Holy Spirit. John Owen, a Welsh theologian who came later than the Reformers themselves, tells us that the gospel "keeps the heart always in deep humility, in abhorrence to sin, and in self abasement. . . . It keeps the heart humble, lowly, sensible to sin, and broken on that account."[15]

Whatever your background, if you lack feelings of "abhorrence to [your own] sin" and are not "broken" because of it, then though you may have a grasp of the doctrines of grace, you are no longer in touch with the Spirit of grace. On the other hand, if you find yourself in the first joyful flush of a refreshing experience of the Holy Spirit on you—beware! It is not a sanctifying experience. You need to learn about the law of sin in your members. I cannot do better than to quote from Owen again, as he comments on Romans 7:21:

Notice that Paul says four things in this verse. First, he says that sin is a "law." Second, he describes this discovery: "I *find* a law." Third, he indicates a context of this discovery, "when I would do good." Fourth, he specifies the state and activity of this law of sin: "evil is present with me."[16]

Owen proceeds to explain what he means by each of these four. When he calls sin a "law" he is claiming that it "directs and commands, regulating the mind and will in many ways." Sin is in control. Hence our struggle, hence our defeats and frustrations. It "denotes the reality and the nature of sins, . . . signifies the power and efficacy of sins."

But you have to discover this "law" for yourself. You may be sublimely unaware of your sins, or untroubled by them. Owen reminds us that in verse 21 Paul *finds* the law in himself. You may know in theory about the law, even agree that it exists. "But to experience and find it for oneself is another matter."[17]

So how and when do you find it? You do so "when you would do good," Paul says. Eugene Peterson's translation of the verse is worth quoting:

It happens so regularly that it's predictable. The moment I decide to do good, sin is there to trip me up. I truly delight in God's commands, but it's pretty obvious that not all of me joins in that delight. Parts of me covertly rebel, and just when I least expect it, they take charge.[18]

My friend Steve's grouchiness illustrates this law. When I encountered him six months after his "spiritual drunkenness," I did not ask the Spirit to fall again on him in power. Recognizing his difficulty for what it was, I dealt with its underlying causes.

What Happened to Steve

Let me get back to the Toronto conference where Steve sat on the front row, between Lorrie and me. What exactly happened there?

During the "ministry time," Lorrie and I joined with Joy Best (the wife of Gary Best, who pastors the Langley Vineyard) to pray for grouchy Steve. As we asked the Lord to guide us in prayer, for some reason I thought of Brazil and the terrible witchcraft cults there. My frame of mind was such that I had zero expectation of the Lord's great power; however, automatically raising my hand I cried, "I come against Macumba[19] in the name of Jesus!"

I did not expect that anything would happen. But immediately Steve's chair shot backward, hitting an empty chair behind it and ramming that chair into the knees of a man seated in the third row. The man grinned, seeming to enjoy the fun. Steve's face twisted diabolically, and he began to retch. We shoved Kleenex into his hands.

Later I accompanied Steve home, convinced that there was more to be dealt with. As we prayed further, I spoke against the Black Jehovah (another Brazilian cult). Steve showed further demonic manifestations, but the oppressing demons quickly departed. His joy was restored immediately, for his will had already been set in the direction of doing good.

Evil dwells in our flesh, serving as an access point for external evil. It will dwell in our flesh until we die and our bodies rot. Though we "will be raised from the grave incorruptible" (1 Cor 15:42 KJV), we must wait till then to be completely rid of inner evil. It resides in our rotting flesh (that is why our bodies rot)—the same flesh God created free from the curse. It was when we listened to darkness that our problems began. Rotting and rottenness came.

In Galatians Paul says, "For the sinful nature desires what is contrary to the Spirit, and the Spirit what is contrary to the sinful nature. They are in conflict with each other, so that you do not do what you want" (5:17).

The Land of Beulah

I wish I could tell you there is a state in this life where we shall forever be free from sin. But I cannot, for it is not true. In *Pilgrim's Progress* John Bunyan describes a state that he calls "the Enchanted Ground" and "the Country of Beulah." I have the feeling that he is speaking of an experience in which heaven is much more real to a Christian than it has ever before been. Some Christians do have such experiences. But even here the sinful nature is still in one's flesh; it is only that one's peace and vision of what is coming seems to leave one freer than ever from sin's pull. Bunyan writes,

Here [the pilgrims] were within sight of the City they were going to: also here met them some of the inhabitants thereof; for in this land the shining ones commonly walked, because it was upon the borders of heaven. In this land also the contract between the bride and the bridegroom was renewed; yea, here, as the bridegroom rejoiceth over the bride, so did their God rejoice over them.[20]

It may be some time yet before you and I enter the Country of Beulah. I know it exists, for I catch glimpses of it from time to time. In the meantime I wrestle against this evil in my flesh. And with dear John Owen I say to you,

Our enemy is not only *upon us*, as it was with Samson, but it is also *in us*. So if we would not dishonor God and His Gospel, if we would not scandalize the saints of God, if we would not avoid our own conscience and endanger our own soul, if we would not grieve the Holy Spirit, then we must stay alert to our danger.[21]

8

RIGHTEOUSNESS
—NOW!

And that [sexually immoral, idolaters, thieves . . .]
is what some of you were. But you were washed, you
were sanctified, you were justified in the
name of the Lord Jesus Christ and by the Spirit of our God.
(1 Corinthians 6:11)

No blood, no altar now,
The sacrifice is o'er;
No flame, no smoke ascends on high,
The lamb is slain no more;
But richer blood has flowed from nobler veins
To purge the soul from guilt, and cleanse the reddest stains.
(Horatius Bonar, "No Blood, No Altar Now")

GOD MADE YOU RIGHTEOUS THE MOMENT YOU BECAME A CHRISTIAN. HE *righteoused* you. He also sanctified you, in the sense of making you fit for his personal use.[1]

There are two senses in which the word *sanctification* is used in Scripture. First Corinthians 6:11 tells us, "You were washed, you were sanctified, you were justified in the name of the Lord Jesus Christ and by the Spirit of our God." Paul is telling us that our sanctification happened in the past, that we are now sanctified.

This meaning of the term—made fit for use by God—is the one used most commonly in Scripture. Why, then, do I depart from it? I do so because when most Christians use the term they think of *progress in* sanctification, and this too is a biblical meaning of the term. Paul, for instance, writes in his second letter to Timothy, "If a man cleanses himself, . . . he will be an instrument for noble purposes, made holy, useful to the Master and prepared to do any good work" (2:21). Here we plainly have a different use of the word. We begin to see that sanctification, the process by which we become holy, is not complete when God saves us. We must cleanse ourselves from certain associations. Effort is involved. If we do what Paul says we will be made holy, "useful to the Master and prepared to do any good work."

Our everyday experience teaches us the same thing: we know perfectly well that our thoughts, words and actions are at times anything but holy. Paul warns about this by describing his own experience in Romans 7. Here he discusses what we call *carnality:* our strange proclivity to sinful behavior. I have already quoted Eugene Peterson's interpretation of verse 18: "It happens so regularly that it's predictable. The moment I decide to do good, sin is there to trip me up. I truly delight in God's commands, but it's pretty obvious that not all of me joins in that delight. Parts of me covertly rebel, and just when I least expect it, they take charge" (TM).

Righteousness

I find that many Christians who struggle to be holy are unconsciously trying to get even with their conscience. Righteousness comes when by faith you trust Jesus as Savior and Lord. You are righteous *because God says so.* He is not pretending that something is true when it is not. He sees you *in Christ.* He sees you as you really are in eternity's reckoning. Christ fulfilled the law for us (Rom 10:4; Gal 2:21), and we are now in him, in total unity with him. In love and mercy Christ has already done all that is necessary. Until from the soles of your feet to the crown of your head you know that God has made you righteous, you will not make progress in holiness. Haunted by the Accuser, you will keep trying to do what Christ has already done.

I tried to explain this last Sunday to a young man, telling him that the death of Christ had made him righteous. He responded, in effect, "Yes, yes—I know that. There's no problem there." But there *was* a problem. He knew it intellectually and theologically. But the truth, at least at that moment, eluded his whole being. Righteousness is a given. You wear a white robe to prove it (Rev 19:8). God sees it even if you do not. God has declared you righteous, and whatever God declares is so. Righteousness, then, is the doorway to holiness.

Rediscovering Your Righteousness

Years ago I took part in committee meetings at Tyndale House, Cambridge. When I was there I attended an evening Bible study led by the Reverend Alan Stibbs. Listening to his scholarly exposition of

Revelation 12:1-12, I was gripped by a sense that what I was hearing was one of the great keys to Christian living. Yet the essence of the exposition eluded me. I couldn't quite grasp what he was saying.

When I returned to Buenos Aires, where I was working, I was haunted by a repetitive dream. I kept dreaming it was the last night before my final examination in medicine. In my dream I had not read a single textbook. Piles of never-opened books surrounded me. I was struggling desperately to make up for my procrastination. The clock relentlessly registered the rapid passage of the night hours. I stared at shiny, virgin pages of a physiology textbook, laboring to absorb its contents. Constantly I would have to reread what I had already gone over, for my mind wandered, adding to my terror. Finally I would wake, sweating and trembling.

So vivid each dream seemed that the terror of a future exam still haunted me as I came into waking consciousness. Several minutes would pass before I began to realize that I had passed my finals long before. I was already a partly trained surgeon. So why the dreams? What did they mean? Was God trying to tell me something?

I wrote to Alan Stibbs describing my dreams. He replied in a closely hand-written letter whose contents I devoured. He explained that my dream reflected a haunted conscience: *I didn't know how righteous I really was!* Again he explained the significance of blood in Scripture.

As I read his letter, my eyes were opened. What had eluded me in Cambridge became clear. Suddenly I knew, *knew* what I had not known even moments before—that God had set me free to walk along the pathway of holiness! In that moment I became aware that there was nothing I wanted more than to pursue holiness. I had no desire to exploit cheap grace. God had set me free, free to be what I wanted to be—holy. Oh, the joy of those days!

Yet such was the ingrained habit of legalism in me that eventually I found myself sometimes slipping back, falling repeatedly under the Accuser's charges, sliding into darkness, until the same lesson was repeated at ever-increasing depths. For biblical truth comes to us by revelation, lighting our darkness. If you are like me, you will learn the same lesson repeatedly.

I remember an early morning many years later. Troubled by my sinfulness, I waited on God in silence. Christ by his Holy Spirit spoke into my spirit the words "But I have already given you my righteousness!"

Before I could stop myself, I cried out, "I don't want your righteousness! *I want my own!*"

Suddenly I realized what I had said. I was stunned by words that had come unbidden from my own mouth. But soon I began to chuckle to myself—and then to worship. I was awed by the wonder of an astonishing love that never tired of teaching me about God's goodness—the goodness of a Father, and the goodness of a Son who delighted in him.

Assurance of Salvation

Throughout history many have agonized over whether God has accepted them. Some have been taught that it is presumptuous to claim assurance of one's salvation. As a physician I have seen appalling fear on some people's faces at the point of death. They viewed death with terror. One man cried out to me in dread as he was dying. We need assurance, an assurance not based on our own merits but on Christ's.

J. I. Packer rightly bases our assurance on the biblical doctrine of adoption.[2] Noting that even the Puritans gave inadequate attention to this doctrine, he argues for the blood-bought right of every Christian to know, with subjective assurance, that they need have no fear of death. Assurance is given to us on the basis of our understanding of Scripture and a loving Father's ability to impart by his Spirit. Nevertheless, Packer says, "Christians who grieve the Spirit by sin, and who fail to seek God with all their heart, must expect to miss the full fruition of this crowning gift of the double witness, just as careless and naughty children stop their parents' smiles and provoke frowns instead."[3]

As a psychiatrist (for I am no theologian) I agree. I have seen too many Christians who, in a deep and sometimes psychotic depression, have lost all sense of assurance. Our very brains, on which we depend so greatly, do not function properly at such times. Our powers of thought are fallen, just like the rest of us. To depend on our ability to think matters through, when to do so is to depend on neurotransmitters in a fallen brain, is folly.

Our logical abilities will always be under attack. The Accuser attacks us "day and night" (Rev 12:10) with accusation. As Tempter-in-Chief he stirs up the law of sin in our members. He will bring confusion so that we cannot grasp the difference between our sins and our sinful*ness*.

The "Law of Sin"

To be made holy, you first had to be made righteous. Why do many Christians walk through their days haunted by vague feelings of guilt? Part of the reason is that they have a vague sense of wrong within. Paul knew that this sense of wrong results from the principle of sin inside us all (Rom 7:21-25). "The law of sin" is the phrase he used to describe our inherited vulnerability to sin. Though our sins may be forgiven, our proclivity to sin—our susceptibility to it—remains in every cell in our bodies. But I see another law at work in the members of my body, "waging war against the law of my mind and making me a prisoner of the law of sin at work within my members" (Rom 7:23).

Christians down the ages have attached great significance to the law of sin. John Owen, the great Puritan theologian, said, "The law of sin is an indwelling principle. It 'dwelleth in me,' confesses the apostle in Romans 7:20. It is 'present with me' (7:21). It is 'in my members' (7:23). It is an indwelling law in my flesh—an inward habit and principle."[4]

Does your conscience haunt you? Do you push back accusing voices that remind you of your past? Or of your moral ugliness? Or even that in some vague way question your present standing before God? Sometimes you may have no recollection of anything you have done that is sin, yet you feel full of guilt, not knowing why. There is a solution.

In the book *Holiness* Bishop J. C. Ryle puts his finger on the reason. He quotes from Robert Traill's sermons: "Nay, a saint in heaven is not more justified than a believer on earth is: *only they know it better*."[5] Nobody in heaven is haunted by qualms of conscience! People there are full of bliss. Our present experience may be little like theirs. We may lack assurance that all is well, may think God must have something against us. Doubts can haunt us. We will "know better" in heaven, but what about now? Do we have to wait till then to know that we are truly righteous? Absolutely not.

Most Christians who aim seriously at holiness fall immediately into the trap of seeking something else—not holiness, but righteousness. They talk holiness but think righteousness, confusing the two. Before you can begin to make any progress whatever in holiness, you have to *know* you are righteous, know that the blood of Christ has made you clean, pure and holy.

But as we have already seen, there are two sides to holiness. Our behavior can be anything but holy. Righteousness is where holiness begins. The choice for each of us lies between righteousness, flagrant sinfulness and legalism. But you wouldn't read this book if you wanted sin. So your personal choice is between legalism and a righteousness you already possess.

The Curse of Legalism

What is legalism? Legalists base their spiritual comfort on their own efforts. Where does legalism come from? How do we get entangled with it? Like the law of sin itself, it comes from the very cells of which we are made. We and all our forebears have been dyed-in-the-wool, defensive legalists.

To be a legalist is, for one thing, to be defensive. All of us retain strong legalist leanings in our hearts. We have a psychological bent toward legalism, because we are forever trying to justify ourselves. The tendency to justify ourselves (to be defensive) is innate in every Christian and every non-Christian. It came with our shame of nakedness.

Let me take the liberty of modernizing the dialogue between God and our first parents in the Garden of Eden. Just imagine Adam and Eve cowering, aprons or no aprons, in the bushes.

GOD:	Who told you that you were naked?
ADAM:	Well, er, you see, this creature that you put with me, she . . .
GOD (to Eve):	So what's your story?
EVE:	Well, like, there was this serpent—and boy, did he fool me . . !

Both were being defensive. Both had already become legalists, for that is what legalists are. Legalists justify themselves and are therefore *self*-righteous. No longer does the love of Christ awe them so much that they spend their days in wonder.

James Denney reminds us of that awesome love of Christ: "If it is our death that Christ died on the cross, there is in the cross the constraint of an infinite love."[6] Paul said the same thing long before Denney: "God demonstrates his own love for us in this: While we were still sinners, Christ died for us" (Rom 5:8).

When we first come to the Savior, most of us are overwhelmed by his love and his extraordinary grace in dying for us. And to know the love of Christ is to overcome legalism. Yet as time passes, somehow God's love in Christ seems to fade in our minds. We grow more conscious of important facts and doctrines—of substitionary atonement or the importance of the faith that justifies. Slowly the greatness of Christ's love for us fades from awareness. It no longer stirs us, though we retain it as a theological fact, tucked away under "doctrine" in our mental files. How could we ever forget? Denney says, "*He* bore *our* sins, *he* died *our* death. It is *so* his love constrains us."[7]

Constrains us? To do what? To be able to enter our full inheritance. To worship and adore. That love must constrain us still—must still draw us. It is not just the theological understanding of the atonement, but the love that constrained him to do such a thing for us—to divest himself of glory, to be born in a stable, to live the life of an earthly nobody, to be mocked, despised, unjustly flogged like a criminal and then unjustly crucified between to real criminals. *That* was love. He despised all he went through—the pain, the utter, unspeakable shame, the horror of a great darkness. His eyes were resting on us. He wanted to free us. He was inspired by what he was determined to win for us. Let our eyes then be on him, on "Jesus . . . who for the joy set before him endured the cross, scorning its shame, and sat down at the right hand of the throne of God" (Heb 12:2).

Two Dangers

When I discovered Satan's strategy as the Accuser, what astonished me was the experience of freedom—*my* freedom—my freedom to be holy. To be frank, it startled me! I, John White, was free to walk in holiness.

Immediately I thought of Paul's expression in Romans 6: "What shall we say, then? Shall we go on sinning so that grace may increase? By no means! We died to sin; how can we live in it any longer? Or don't you know that all of us who were baptized into Christ Jesus were baptized into his death?" (vv. 1-3). This chapter follows Paul's long and careful argument on the basis of justification. But immediately he knows how some people will argue—perhaps some in scorn and others in delight. An awareness of God's grace can make us careless about sin. We can respond by saying, "Grace has made me free! My sins in the past and the present *and the future* are all forgiven." Such an attitude does not promote sanctity. On the other hand, the accusations of Satan can turn us, as we have seen, into frustrated legalists.

So far in this chapter we have been discussing our lack of awareness of our righteousness and how the guilt-producing attacks of the Accuser are the source of our difficulty. This will also be the theme of the next chapter. But before I continue, let me remind you that we are saved *into a family.* Whereas the law was once our problem, now the family is! We can grieve the Holy Spirit by our sin, which must be confessed and repented of.

The incident where Jesus washes the disciples' feet in the Gospel of John is profoundly symbolic. Jesus was doing more than washing feet. His action on this occasion is both didactic and practical. It represents his love to the apostles, even to Judas, and it teaches the nature of authority and at the same time has a profound bearing on sanctification.

Curiously, in John's account of the Last Supper he mentions nothing about the breaking of the bread and the wine, which the Synoptic Gospels feature prominently. Yet in the sixth chapter of John's Gospel Jesus has already spoken of himself as the bread of life. The symbolism of breaking bread and drinking wine at the Last Supper had been suggested to the bewildered multitudes when Jesus spoke of exercising faith in him. To do so is to "eat the flesh of the Son of Man and [to] drink his blood" (see Jn 6:25-59).

On the night of the Last Supper the apostles may have been physically and emotionally uncomfortable. Our knowledge of customs of the time is considerable, but not great enough to allow us to know exactly how they would have felt. Not every host of the time made sure his guests' feet were washed; the custom was noticeably omitted when Jesus visited a certain Pharisee (Lk 7:44-46). Still, the disciples may have been accustomed to having someone wash their feet for them. Along with mild discomfort from dusty feet, each may have had another kind of discomfort, thinking, *Well, I'm not the one to do it!* (Washing feet was a servant's job, and servants were cheap.) R. V. G. Tasker suggests, "It may well be that it was the strife that had arisen among the apostles at the supper table as to which of them should be accounted greatest, that led Jesus to decide upon this particular method of emphasizing the truth of His words, 'But I am among you as one who serves.' "[8]

Two things are important as we try to understand what is going on here. First, Jesus is teaching. The foot washing is a *didactic* occasion. But it is more than didactic: it is a supreme expression of love. "Having loved his own who were in the world, he now showed them the full extent of his love" (Jn 13:1).

Jesus is teaching that authority comes to us when our prime motive is to serve others. And the second important lesson concerns our sanctification. Let us join the apostles as Jesus, dressed as a servant and wearing only a loincloth and carrying a linen towel, approaches Peter.

He came to Simon Peter, who said to him, "Lord, are you going to wash my feet?"

Jesus replied, "You do not realize now what I am doing, but later you will understand."

"No," said Peter, "you shall never wash my feet." (vv. 6-8)

Remember, this is taking place at the Passover feast. Jesus may have been teaching the apostles (who still failed to understand fully) about the significance of the Passover and the ceremonial use of blood. When the angel of death and judgment came to Egypt, the Israelites had been protected by blood, the evidence of death, smeared on their doorposts and lintels (Ex 12:7, 13). In the same way Jesus himself would by his death abolish death's rule, to which humankind had been in bondage. But the apostles were in no condition to grasp the meaning of all that was happening around them and to them.

Imagine yourself in the group of apostles. I can understand why the apostle John, for instance, allowed Jesus to wash his feet, but I am puzzled by the others. My reaction would have been like Peter's. Had I been an apostle, no way would I have permitted the King of Glory to wash my feet. It would have seemed utterly inappropriate.

But Jesus has said something mysterious: "You do not realize now what I am doing, but later you will understand." What does he mean? Clearly, he is referring to his victory on the cross over death. That is what would accomplish our salvation.

Jesus also says, "Unless I wash you, you have no part with me" (v. 8). The words are frightening. Let me colloquialize them. "Peter, this is it. If I do not wash your feet, this is the end of our togetherness."

Just what is he saying? Certainly he is not saying that Peter would lose his salvation, but that he would lose a sense of intimate fellowship with Christ. And his warning has meaning for our own daily walk. Life in a sinful world inevitably brings defilement. It is not the defilement of mere contact with sinful people, but of a thousand little thoughts and reactions in response to them, to conversations, to all I have heard and seen on TV or in newspapers. I live in a defiling world, and I have been defiled. I need time with Christ. I need to take my shoes and socks off and let him wash my feet. To wash them properly, he has to see where the dirt is. In other words, I have to let him see me, to see the defilement in my heart. Defilement always involves my sin. He can perceive that sin better than I. I need not search, but he can—if I give him time. And it takes time.

The foot-washing hands of Jesus are real, tender and loving. Love pours through his fingertips. He graciously kneels to be my servant in this, just as he knelt before Peter.

"Then, Lord," Simon Peter replied, "not just my feet but my hands and my head as well!"

Jesus answered, "A person who has had a bath needs only to wash his feet; his whole body is clean. And you are clean, though not every one of you." For he knew who was going to betray him, and that was why he said not every one was clean. (Jn 13:9-11) When Christ "righteoused" us, we had our bath. We need no other. As God looks on us he sees the result of that bath. But John Calvin, treating this same question, says,

> The term feet, therefore, is metaphorically applied to all the passions and cares with which we are brought into contact with the world; for, if the Holy Spirit occupied every part of us, we would no longer have anything to do with the pollutions of the world; but now, by

that part in which we are carnal, we creep on the ground . . . and
. . . are to some extent unclean.

If sanctification is to proceed in us, we must have a thorough grasp of
the relationship between righteousness and sanctification. Calvin continues, "Thus Christ always finds in us something to cleanse. What is
here spoken of is not the forgiveness of sins, but the renewal, by which
Christ, by gradual and uninterrupted succession, delivers his followers
entirely from the sinful desires of the flesh."[9]

Some Christians today are attracted by teachings that overemphasize
the fact that we are forgiven for "sins past, present and future" and
neglect to remind us that we are now members of the family of God.
It is perfectly true that we are forgiven, and God understands that we
sin; but our sin still affects our relationship with him. For instance, we
are instructed not to grieve the Holy Spirit (Eph 4:30). Sin will never
rob us of our family membership, but it does affect relationships within
the family circle. We grieve the Holy Spirit, and we discover that
fellowship with him is no longer the same.

I can always approach God—boldly. If I take the time to dwell in
his presence, especially if I begin to reflect on the price he paid for my
redemption, he will show me any sources of estrangement between us.
The very removal of sinful dirt may bring pain—perhaps great pain—
but more often it brings relief and comfort, for our God is wonderfully
gentle.

He may not only show us sin but pluck the roots of it right out. Or
he may leave us to struggle with it. But it is absolutely essential that
we continue to bring our sin before him. *Foot washing must continue.*
If it does not, our sanctification will stall.

In John's first epistle, his exhortation is to Christians—to family
members—when he says, "If we confess our sins, he is faithful and just
and will forgive us our sins and purify us from all unrighteousness. If
we claim we have not sinned, we make him out to be a liar and his
word has no place in our lives" (1 Jn 1:9-10).

Christ wants to minister to you in love. His love, if you will let it,
will soften your heart, so warming and reassuring you that legalism
becomes an absurd alternative. Joy will spring up in you once again.
And, most important of all, you will find yourself running boldly and

with complete confidence into the presence of the Father, knowing that his arms are reaching out to you in love. He knows, even if you have forgotten, that the death of Christ is enough. Enough for him. Enough for us.

PART 2

THE WAY
OF
HOLINESS

---

*B*Y "THE WAY OF HOLINESS" I MEAN THE SORT OF PATH BY WHICH WE pursue holiness. To pursue holiness is to pursue God himself, to seek his face. He invites all Christians to do this very thing, and has made provision for us, since he himself wants intimacy with us. We experience frustration because we have little experience of the pathway.

This part of the book is a beginners' guide. It is not for those who for years have been entering ever more deeply into these things. And because beginners are sometimes a little suspicious, I must focus on what Scripture says.

I begin in chapter nine with those conditions God seems to demand if he is to communicate effectively with us. In chapter ten I deal with an old classic that, though written long before the Great Awakening began, had a profound influence on some of its leaders. It is Henry

Scougall's book *The Life of God in the Soul of Man.* The idea of divine life within us is profoundly important. In chapter eleven I go on to examine a complementary idea found in 2 Corinthians 3:18. Various translations interpret the most important phrase in this verse differently. Thus it is that again we are faced with the question of scholarship. It is a truism that while we cannot do without scholars, they also cause many of our difficulties. In any case, I try to show why I opt for particular translations of this very important verse.

In chapters twelve and thirteen I attempt to take a look at the whole church. Holiness is not merely a question of you, me and God. It has to do with the corporate body uniting Jew and Gentile, Catholic and Protestant, charismatic and noncharismatic—to name only a few currently separated groups. We come into holiness *together.*

9

WAITING ON GOD

Speak, Lord, in the stillness, while I wait on Thee;
Hushed my heart to listen in expectancy.
Speak, O blessed Master, in this quiet hour,
Let me see Thy face, Lord, feel Thy touch of pow'r.
For the words Thou speakest, "they are life" indeed;
Living Bread from heaven, now my spirit feed!
(E. May Grimes, "Speak, Lord, in the Stillness")

Prayer is the peace of our spirit, the stillness of our thoughts,
the evenness of our recollection,
the sea of our meditation, the rest of our cares,
the calm of our tempest. (Jeremy Taylor)

*T*HE TITLE OF THIS CHAPTER, "WAITING ON GOD," MAKES ME THINK OF THE impatience I experience when someone keeps me waiting. I glance repeatedly at my watch, restlessly pace up and down, filled with questions like *Why can't he (she) be on time? Where can he (she) be? What's taking so long?* Yet when I meet whomever I am waiting for, I push my impatience down in the relief and joy of seeing them.

God waits for us. And when we pray we are supposed to wait for and on him. He is a person, and if I cannot control the comings and goings of other people, I certainly cannot control God's. Of course in a sense he's always near, but we need him to be near relationally. Yet God sometimes keeps me waiting.

In the restlessness and rush of our souls and of the age we live in, we need to calm down and be still. Many Christians would think little of the quote at the head of this chapter from Jeremy Taylor, which I came across in a book of religious quotes. *Is* prayer "the peace of our spirit"? Whether Taylor is right or wrong, we will not get anywhere in prayer until we find "the peace of our spirit, the stillness of our thoughts" and all the rest. Peace and stillness are not only desirable. They are essential.

Just as God takes the initiative in every aspect of our holiness, so in this aspect of holiness he must precede us. Prayer should always be a response to God. Admittedly he sometimes does something to *make* us cry out to him—but he's still the one who starts it. Prayer that God did not start is not prayer at all. Prayer is our response to him. Most people, if asked what a holy person is like, would say that a holy person would "pray a lot." They are probably right. But we must understand that the motive for holy people's prayer is not to get holier, but the fact that they find peace and joy during times of prayer. For them prayer is a delight. They come to God because they know he can be trusted. They know his person. They are like people who cannot stand a stuffy room and stride to the window to fling it open.

Is prayer *supposed* to be a delight? Is it supposed to be "the peace of our spirit, the stillness of our thoughts"? Certainly I believe it commonly begins there. What does Scripture actually teach?

Biblical Stillness
Scripture associates stillness and silence with prayer. One of the Old Testament words for stillness is *dāmam*, which literally means "still as stone." Psalm 4:4 tells us, "In your anger do not sin; when you are on your beds, search your hearts and be silent." "Silent" here is a translation of *dāmam*—still. But why be still? Why search our hearts?

The verse begins with "In your anger . . ." Apart from anything else, anger is a very uncomfortable feeling. It prevents sleep, spoils digestion, impairs relationships and raises blood pressure. Storms are going on inside you when you are angry. Occasionally *dāmam* carries the sense of dread, for our stillness is to be in God's presence. His drawing near can be fearful. But it can also have the sense of being for our own benefit.

One of my favorite hymns includes this stanza:
Drop Thy still dews of quietness,
Till all our strivings cease;
Take from our souls the strain and stress,
And let our ordered lives confess
The beauty of Thy peace.[1]
Before we sort other people out we need to have ourselves sorted out. Before we can make effective use of our anger we need God to tell us

how. He needs to "breathe through the heats of our desire" his coolness and his balm. And for that to happen we need to learn how to become *dāmam,* still as stone, that he may speak.

But I have stilled and quieted my soul;
like a weaned child with its mother,
like a weaned child is my soul within me. (Ps 131:2)

To still my heart implies there is a need—that my heart is not still. Our thoughts can so easily become wild rides on a bolting "high horse."

My heart is not proud, O LORD,
my eyes are not haughty;
I do not concern myself with great matters
or things too wonderful for me. (Ps 131:1)

When God has stilled you after periods of turbulence, he brings you to the point where you are indeed like a weaned child. An inner stillness comes, the stillness of lying in his arms. It is a prelude to peace.

When you find yourself unable to gain a sense of God's presence, remember that anger could be a cause. Search your heart for anger. If you should find it, tell the Lord, "I'd forgotten I was angry." Or, "Lord, I'm angry. I've tried not to be, but I can't stop being angry, so please help me!" Knowing his love for you helps. Some anger, I know, is so deep that we no longer feel it. But in his time and way, God can reveal it.

One New Testament word for stillness is *hēsychios*—still, undisturbed, quiet. Peter uses it in 1 Peter 3:4: "the unfading beauty of a gentle and *quiet* spirit, which is of great worth in God's sight."

Another New Testament word is *hēsychia,* the absence of bustle and fuss. Paul uses this word in 2 Thessalonians. Certain members of the church had too little to occupy their time and energy. They were altogether too interested in other people's affairs—and not in the most helpful way. "Such people we command and urge in the Lord Jesus Christ to *settle down* and earn the bread they eat" (2 Thess 3:12). Anger is not the only thing that creates inner storms. God cannot speak to us when criticisms and gossip echo loudly through the chambers of our hearts. We need *hēsychia,* inner tranquillity.

Again and again in Scripture we find mention of the need for such a stillness. So again, take time (you may have quite a struggle) to detach yourself from "busybody" thoughts.

Consider Isaiah 30:15, which shows how quietness, faith, repentance and trust all work together:

This is what the Sovereign LORD, the Holy One of Israel, says:

"In repentance [*šûb*—a returning] and rest [*naḥaṯ*—resting, lighting down] is your salvation,

in quietness [*šāqaṭ*—repose, stillness] and trust [*bāṭaḥ*] is your strength,

but you would have none of it."

God requires—but never forces—us to return repeatedly in repentance, rest, stillness and trust. But my favorite calls to quietness are in the Psalms.

Be Still and Know

Be still [*rāp̄âh*—to let go], and know that I am God;

I will be exalted among the nations,

I will be exalted in the earth. (Ps 46:10)

Under what circumstances am I to "be still and know"? What do these words mean? Surely I must be still and know in all circumstances—that is, if I can. But how?

First let me address the circumstances the psalmist contemplates in Psalm 46. In verses 2-4 he contemplates the possibility of catastrophic and frightening events in creation—the earth giving way, mountains quaking and even falling into the sea, the roaring and foaming of waters. When catastrophe of this magnitude strikes—and these days the news constantly seems to bring us such tidings—even the most trusting of us feels our courage draining away. The unspoken question is "What would happen if . . . ?"

Therefore we will not fear, though the earth give way

and the mountains fall into the heart of the sea,

though its waters roar and foam

and the mountains quake with their surging. (vv. 2-3)

Such events make us fear. As I write, I look at TV pictures of floods in the Missouri basin and the Mississippi. As I contemplate similar recent catastrophes in Bangladesh, and as I reflect that these things are God's judgments, I am deeply troubled. Even though I had been praying that God would bring his righteous judgments on earth, having witnessed the coming of some of those judgments Lorrie and I wept yesterday as we prayed, struggling in metaphorical waters of horror ourselves.

Yet the psalmist defiantly declares, in effect, "Therefore we will not fear—whatever may happen to the created order." But there is more to come. In addition to natural catastrophes, verse 6 contemplates international disturbances: "Nations are in uproar, kingdoms fall."

It is the same as I write. Just now in the former Yugoslavia, as in Israel and Lebanon, terrible violence reveals the utter helplessness of earthly governments. Both varieties of disturbance—in creation and in the horrors of war—are expressions of divine judgment.

Yet the psalm begins with solid comfort. It is written to show us the principles of finding quietness, stillness, peace in the midst of a world in tumult, of finding comfort even as wars rage around us, and even when our own children perish in the midst of them. In the center of calamity we are not helpless. We may weep, but there is something we can do. We have somewhere to fly to. We may be powerless to control creation or to solve international crises, but we are to fly to God for shelter. However frightening earthly events may be, in our terror we have a refuge to escape to. As fear paralyzes our limbs and helplessness freezes our brains, we can and must run. We do not run *from* catastrophes but *to* God. "God is our refuge and strength, an ever-present help in trouble" (v. 1). We who long to be sanctified must learn this.

But where do we find God when he seems so remote, so very distant? In the time when Psalm 46 was written, he had chosen to locate himself in Zion. In contrast to the waters that roared and foamed, the psalmist could write of "a river whose streams make glad the city of God, the holy place where the Most High dwells" (v. 4). Yet there is no river beside Jerusalem. "Zion's river" is a different kind of river, not unlike Ezekiel's (Ezek 47:1-12). This river flows from the presence, the person, the character of God and the finished work of his Son. It is a river of life, mediated to us by the Spirit of God, and can gush forth from us to others.

I must not disguise the fact that the river is sometimes not easy to discover. But it is there.

The real message of the psalm is repeated twice, in a sort of refrain—a glorious affirmation of truth found in verse 7 and again in verse 11: "The LORD Almighty is with us; the God of Jacob is our fortress." God is with us. He is close to us, whether our feelings tell us so or not. He is a refuge.

Reaching Out for God

God is not, and never was, exclusively confined to temples that human beings construct, which was the thrust of Paul's address on Mars Hill. "He made all nations . . . so that they would search for God and perhaps grope for him and find him" (Acts 17:26-27 NRSV). Whatever we may feel or not feel, God is "not far from each one of us" (v. 27).

Paul's speech was given to a bunch of philosophers and would-be philosophers. Presumably they were not overwhelmed by catastrophe all around them. When one is not facing great difficulty, the whole picture is different. Under those circumstances we are to *grope after God till we find him.* He is at all times close, whether he feels close or not.

So grope. You are in the dark? Do not pull your feelers in, but put them out and grope after him. Are you not his? Do you not bear his image? Are you not born of the Spirit? Then stir yourself! Seek him! Give neither him nor yourself any rest until you find him! For God and God alone is our refuge and our strength. Far from being distant, he is our *ever-present help.*

Letting Things Fall

When tragedy overwhelms you, as described in Psalm 46, matters are different. That is why the psalmist's instructions differ from the apostle's. The psalmist contemplates raging seas and the heartless and cruel hate of foreign armies. Yet he says, "Be still and know!"

The Hebrew word he uses for being still is *rāpâh*. It means to let something go, to cause it to fall, to drop it. Other meanings suggested are to relax, to slacken one's hold. One's hold on what? We must release our idiotic and purely imaginary need to be in control, if not of events, then certainly of our own lives.

When you find yourself in tumultuous circumstances, it is easy to think of nothing but what surrounds you. Your thoughts go round and round about how to solve the problem. Sometimes things seem so appalling that you give up in a wrong sense—in despair. Yet still your thoughts pursue the same ghastly merry-go-round, driving you even deeper into hopelessness.

Rāpâh! Let those thoughts go! Deliberately detach yourself from them. Disconnect. Learn how to uncouple yourself from the horrors that obsess you. God is near you, but you will not experience his nearness as long as you let those thoughts run you into a state of panic or despair. *You can let them go!* So loose your hold. Do not cling any longer to obsessive thoughts. As long as you do not disconnect, that is exactly what you are doing—clinging to an unreal scenario that does not include the presence of your real refuge.

The Beginning of Prayer

Many years ago I wrote a book about the great prayers in the Bible.[2] I was convinced from a study of the Scriptures that real prayer begins when we hear God. He has not ceased to speak. Prayer arises out of what he quickens to us from his Word and by his Spirit. Now I am more convinced of this than ever. It is God's own voice that brings alive our prayer and the Scriptures, so that they quicken our pulses.

Hearing God does take persistence. For the past two mornings I have read assigned morning portions from the Scriptures. They are supposed to bring me joy, but I found them distinctly depressing, for they were passages about the sins and failures of God's people. Each time I thought, *How very unprofitable!* I was not interested in doing what Scripture Union teaches—to "note what sins are to be avoided in the passage." I wanted joy!

So I asked for joy. And it was as though God responded, "Read the passage more carefully. Have confidence that I will speak. Remember my Name. Remember my promises to you." I went back to reread, and—you've guessed it: God started speaking, bringing peace and joy into my heart.

We are so frightened of the possibility of trusting our subjective feelings more than Scripture that we often bury our feelings or try desperately to control them—even though such efforts fail utterly. Yet by some inner sense we may in that moment begin to grope our way in God's direction. He is not far away. Prayer is a learned art. No one can fill themselves with real joy or real peace. To find the Savior is to find peace and rest. For *he is our peace!*

Peace can be found. It may leave us for days at a time, but it can be sought, because *he* can be sought. Let me say again that to seek holiness is to seek God himself.

Inner Turbulence

Are you sure you are in control? If so, beware! I have known God so to disturb the tranquillity of men and women that storms of passion are unleashed within them. They press their lips together as they fight inner storms crashing ceaselessly against rocks and walls of stone within them. God can create storms. He can smash walls and rocks—and will.

Storms are distressing, whether they are the storms of warring nations or storms at sea. "Lord, save us! We're going to drown!" the disciples cried out during a storm on the Sea of Galilee. The storm on the lake produced a storm in their hearts—yet God can still either as we seek him.

[You] formed the mountains by your power,
having armed yourself with strength,
[you] stilled the roaring of the seas,
the roaring of their waves,
and the turmoil of the nations. (Ps 65:6-7)

The word translated "stilled" in verse 7 is actually a participle meaning to soothe, to restrain. The God who can still the seas can certainly calm the teacup tempest of your own heart. Even when God chooses not to restrain the war and tumult around us, we must grope through labyrinthine tunnels of doubt to where he awaits us. There he will soothe and restrain the tumult in our hearts.

Earlier in this chapter I discussed the rushing river of anxious thoughts. Sometimes we need a little practice in "sitting among the reeds" as we let the river sweep by. It does take practice. You should not try to fight your thoughts. Just let them go their merry way. Jump off them, and get in among the reeds. And if you find yourself clinging to any bit of driftwood that comes floating by, then let it go and let the current carry it away. You will never stop the current of your thoughts, so do not try! You don't have to. You can learn to be quiet among the stillness of the reeds. Practice doing so once or twice a week.

All of us must break free from the tendency to cram more and more activity into each day. How you do this is up to you. God calls you to be still and quiet. Take your pick: his stillness or your tumult and rush.

10

THE LIFE
OF GOD
IN THE SOUL
OF MAN

Is not life more important than food,
and the body more important than clothes?
(Matthew 6:25)

*H*ENRY SCOUGALL BECAME A PROFESSOR OF DIVINITY AT ABERDEEN University at an early age. He lived only from 1650 to 1678. In his twenty-seventh year, shortly before his death, he wrote a work called *The Life of God in the Soul of Man*—a title I have borrowed for this chapter. Scougall did not write it as a book, but as a gentle and courteous letter to a friend. Later published in book form, it profoundly affected many Christian leaders in the years that followed. It is recognized as a classic statement about holiness. George Whitefield's life was transformed by it. The front cover of my own copy of Scougall bears a quotation from Whitefield: "I never knew what true religion was till God sent me this excellent treatise."

Scougall's book articulates an important principle: *You conquer sin by feeding life*. To struggle against sin in your own strength is futile. You fight sin best by feeding the life of God in you.

We can think of God's life in various ways—as biological, for example, or as fire. Think now of fire. When a fire burns dim and the embers threaten to die, you blow on it. You also feed it with dry fuel. So it is with divine life. Even though God's part in your sanctification is more important than yours, you share the responsibility to keep the blaze going. You need to stir up this most precious of all gifts, the gift of divine life that has been given you.

Or think of life in a plant. I am the most pathetic of gardeners, but I know that you attack plant diseases best by preventing them, by feeding each plant the amount of light, water and nutrients it requires. The life is already there. That life is a better fighter than you will ever be. Your main job is to supply the components of growth. And you conquer sin the same way.

Earthly fires go out and earthly plants die, but the life of God in your soul never will. Our love may burn low, stifled in part by sinful guilt and neglect, but the fire will be there underneath. Once tended, the fire will burn bright again. So it is most important, if we would conquer sin, to attend to the divine life God gave us—and to cry out to him desperately if need be.

As Scougall explains, spiritual life, in contrast to natural life, "stands in . . . mastery over our natural inclinations, that they may never be able to betray us to those things we know to be blameable."[1] It is the test of truth again—the test that real truth frees you from sin. Jesus came to earth to give us life: "I have come that they may have life, and have it to the full" (Jn 10:10). As the life within us increases, the measure of our holiness will increase along with it.

What We Lost in the Fall

Before we sinned in Adam we had two sorts of life, *natural* (or biological) life and *divine* life. We were hybrids. Biological life includes the life of the soul. Our spirits are different. At the Fall, however, we lost God's fellowship. And to lose fellowship with God is to die. Our spirits were still present in our bodies, but they had lost the capacity to know God. In that sense we "died," for *true life is knowing God.*

Life is the knowledge of God, not mere intelligence and the capacity to reproduce our kind. Our first parents sinned, and as Ezekiel reminds us, God's word to us is "For every living soul belongs to me, the father as well as the son—both alike belong to me. The soul who sins is the one who will die" (Ezek 18:4).

For Adam and Eve there was to be no more walking in the Garden with God, talking, listening, sharing. That life, and with it our capacity for fellowship, was gone. The divine life had been extinguished in human beings, though the potential for it remained. In our gospel presentations we make much of Paul's words "For all have sinned and fall short of the glory of God" (Rom 3:23).

So we were left with natural, biological life. And even in our biological life the death process had begun. We begin to die, physicians tell us, the moment we are born. This is the kind of life we share with plants and animals, the kind God sustains in all physical organisms. He sustains it for the brief period of our life span. He keeps the hearts of even his enemies beating, supplies us all with food, knows when danger threatens us. No bird falls but his mind registers the fact compassionately. Biological life comes from God alone, and he alone preserves it.

God created biological life. It bears the stamp of his character just as spiritual life does. Therefore biological life, on its own and apart from spiritual life, still carries the mark of deity. It responds to kindness and love. Not only so, but it is capable of returning that love and of being loyal to the giver. Faithfulness and sacrifice are known in the animal world. Dogs are faithful to their masters and mistresses, will often defend them and may even sacrifice their lives to do so. There are, so to speak, "martyr dogs." All warm-blooded creatures defend their young. Members of some species are even faithful to their spouses!

The Need of Searching Our Hearts
People who have biological life but lack divine life can still "approve of what is superior" (Rom 2:18). Desiring to corrupt Christ's kingdom from within, Satan places his agents within it. They are people with the very best of natural biological life. They accept the doctrines of Christianity, but they lack divine life. They have never known repentance. They have faith of a sort, but not saving faith. They may be loyal members of evangelical churches, for in every church—just as in the kingdom of God in general[2]—the wheat and the tares grow together. A "pure" church or assembly, consisting only of believers, cannot continue to exist in that state.[3]

Given that biological life without divine life can give rise to love and faithfulness, we cannot assume that the fact that we are kind and loving people proves our relationship to God. We must search our own hearts diligently to see whether the true life is in us. If we have some, we should make sure that it is properly cared for. We must not become the person who tended everybody else's garden but neglected her own (Song 1:6).

It is not our business to sit on God's throne and preselect those people who are to get to heaven, and it is even less our job to force unbelievers out of our churches. That is what the angels get to do. We are not to judge one another. "Anyone who speaks against his brother or judges him speaks against the law and judges it. When you judge the law, you are not keeping it, but sitting in judgment on it. There is only one Lawgiver and Judge, the one who is able to save and destroy. But you—who are you to judge your neighbor?" (Jas 4:11-12). If we have authority to cast anyone from our midst, it must be those true Christians who have fallen into sin and refuse to accept our offer of help and mercy (see 1 Cor 5:11-13).

True, we may have a sense of who belongs to the Lord and who does not. Yet I suspect we are in for a few surprises when we get to heaven. In any case, our business is to care first for our own souls—to feed the flames, to nourish the plant.

At the beginning of any aircraft flight, parents of young children are instructed that in an emergency they must put their own oxygen masks on first. Think about it. A parent might begin to put the mask first on the child. Attending to the child feels more natural, even more noble. But actually the child's survival depends on that of its parents. The parents must think clearly. In a struggle to get a mask on a frightened child, a parent's oxygen-deprived brain could grow confused. In these circumstances the parent could act very foolishly, even becoming "drunk," and could be the inadvertent cause of the child's death.

In the same way our first concern must be to feed the life within us. In the realm of the spirit, as a general rule, we feed others once our own needs have been cared for.

Divine Life

When God reestablishes contact with our fallen selves, our spirits revive, and we come into spiritual life. What, then, are the special characteristics of divine life? How may I know whether I have it? How may I know whether the life within me suffers from neglect? For if I must search my heart I must know what to look for.

Scougall lists five means by which we can know: "The root of divine life is faith; the chief branches are love to God, charity to man, purity and humility."[4] I believe he is right, for he roughly follows Paul's words in Galatians 5:16-25. Faith, love to God, love to others, purity and humility—we could add certain qualifiers, but this combination alone distinguishes the unique divine life from biological life with its capacity for love and sacrifice. These are the basic characteristics that determine that God's life exists and that its fire is well tended. To these five I would add a sixth, conspicuous in today's church by its absence—the fear of God.

The source of divine life is divinely imparted faith. Scougall obviously learned the doctrine from Paul: "For it is by grace you have been saved, through faith—and this not from yourselves, it is the gift of God—not by works, so that no one can boast" (Eph 2:8-9). "Faith . . . and this *not from yourselves* . . ." Only divinely given, divinely imparted faith preserves us from the flames of hell. The doctrine of the *perseverentia sanctorum,* the perseverance of the saints, tells us that divinely imparted faith is faith that endures to the end. It is the life-giving faith of true Christians.

Let me go over the ground again. To have life, you must have God-given faith. God-given faith produces God-given life inside us. God adopts us as his very own children. More wonderful yet, he does so by implanting his own seed within us:

> For you have been born again, not of perishable seed, but of imperishable, through the living and enduring word of God. (1 Pet 1:23)
>
> No one who is born of God will continue to sin, because God's seed remains in him; he cannot go on sinning, because he has been born of God. (1 Jn 3:9)

Notice the second of these verses particularly: "he cannot go on sinning." That is, the one who is born of God cannot persist in deliberate transgression of God's truth. For whenever true Christians do so—and deliberate sin is always a real possibility—they are in danger of hell again.

You say, "Just hold on a minute! Can a true Christian ever be in danger of hell?" Yes indeed, and I speak as a true Calvinist. To be in danger of hell is not the same as actually being thrown in! You are in danger long before that. The moment Christians disobey they turn hellward.

But once true Christians have turned hellward, they will before long begin to tremble in fear. "Do not be afraid of those who kill the body but cannot kill the soul. Rather, be afraid of the One who can destroy both soul and body in hell" (Mt 10:28). The doctrine of the perseverance of the saints teaches us that the flame of saving faith will be kept burning in God's chosen ones (1 Cor 1:8-9; Phil 1:6; 1 Thess 5:23-24). As R. Kearsley, expressing Calvin's own view, puts it, "The confidence of this faith will be sometimes as a light that flickers and even seems to go out altogether. But it will certainly burst into flame again and burn unextinguished to the end."[5]

Love and Fear Together

For Christians to act in disobedience to God, then, is to pursue a hellward course. Such a course should awaken fear and trembling in us—not fear of hell, but of the One who can cast body and soul there.

The fear of God has almost disappeared from Christian thinking. R. T. Jones warns, "The idea that God is not angry with sinners belongs neither to the OT nor to the NT; it is neither Jewish nor Christian, but an alien intrusion from the Greek world of thought."[6]

Love and fear go together. My enjoyment of the priceless privilege of intimacy with God must always be accompanied by awe in his presence. They who love also fear, and the love and the fear grow in equal proportions—certainly it is so in my experience. Perhaps love will have a perfect work in me in future. Paul knew fear. It was the fear of standing one day in the Presence, knowing he would be required to give an account of his stewardship (2 Cor 5:10).

It used to be fashionable to describe men and women as "God-fearing," but the fashion died out long ago. Paul feared God. I have far more reason than Paul to fear. On more than one occasion as God has drawn near, I have known what could only be described as dread or terror. Yet because I loved him, the love (and the joy that accompanied it) were greater than the terror. I would have been willing to die in those moments, in spite of the dread. I loved the One I feared.

Recently I came near death following a second heart attack. In those moments I knew what I dreaded. It was to meet my God with my task unfinished. I knew I was his, but I want a "Well done," not merely to be saved "as one escaping through the flames" (1 Cor 3:15).

The Source of the Christian's Love

How do we learn to love God?

Children whose parents love them find it easy to love. The only way to love a parent is to be loved by that parent. When a little boy lifts his arms to Mommy to be hugged, there is nothing of self-sacrificing nobility in the love he offers. The child who sucks at her breast wants love too. The child's love is called "need love." And that is where we begin. Love and need are inseparably entwined.

St. Bernard of Clairvaux well knew that love springs from being loved. He went to Christ for what he could get—though some of us consider it ignoble to turn to God for what he will give us. Bernard went like a child for candy, but the candy he sought was love. He knew his heart was empty of it, and he raised it as an unfilled vessel again and again.

> Jesus, Thou joy of loving hearts,
> Thou Fount of Life, Thou Light of men,
> From the best bliss that earth imparts
> We turn unfilled to Thee again.[7]

To know God truly is to be flooded by an overwhelming understanding of his love to us. If there is one lesson that God himself by his Spirit has been teaching me all my life, it is that he loves even me. I did not know how to receive that love, nor could I do so. He had to teach me, and has done so oh, so very gently, as his Spirit has wooed me. To be loved, to be flooded and overwhelmed by that love, is to know God's very heart. J. I. Packer comments, "When Paul says, 'the love of God is shed abroad in our hearts by the Holy Ghost which is given unto us' (Rom 5:5 KJV), he means not love for God, but knowledge of God's love for us."[8]

Those children are confident who know by repeated smiles, hugs, loving correction and tenderness that they are loved. Such children are overwhelmed by love. As Packer puts it, in Romans 5:5 "Paul is not talking about faint and fitful impressions, but of deep and overwhelming ones."[9] To be loved is the key to loving others, as well as to loving God himself.

"Spoiled" children know that being lavished with gifts and having their own way is not love. Intuitively they recognize their parents' indulgence as an unsatisfactory substitute for genuine love. They know something is missing. Their testing of limits and their bad behavior represent a groping after real love.

The loved little child loves Daddy. She does not love an abstract daddy but a real one. The love springs up anew whenever he is present. That is why she toddles eagerly to the door as the key turns: she longs for the presence on the other side of the door. Of course she loves the things that go along with Daddy—presents, stories or the security she takes for granted. But it is the presence that is missed. Presents and security are no substitute for presence and person.

So it is with love of God. Scougall tells us that the love of God is a "delightful and affectionate sense of the divine perfections." But such a sense puts deeper desires into our souls, and Scougall provides insight into those desires. They make "the soul resign and sacrifice itself wholly unto him, desiring above all things to please him, and delighting in nothing so much as in fellowship and communion with him."[10]

Daddy is big and strong. Let Daddy shout angrily, and terror fills the child. If she has always been kindly treated, she will not run away but will cling to Daddy, burying her face in the leg of his trousers or creeping fearfully toward him, ready to climb on his knee at the first opportunity. In the same way, both the love and the fear of God are signs of the life of God within us. Perfect love (God's perfect love to us) will gradually dispel the fear, but I suspect that those who have known no fear are the most impoverished Christians of all.

I mentioned earlier that sometimes we cannot feel our love for God. Most Christians have never sought love from the greatest Lover of all. We sing "Jesus, lover of my soul, let me to thy bosom fly," but fail to seek him, much less to let him love us. We fail to trust his great kindness. We are too dignified. So we drop damp rags on the fires of our love, or douse them with resentment, unforgiveness and pride—or even of a spirit of being tough and managing without God.

Yet Scougall says that the true Christian delights "in nothing so much as in fellowship and communion with him." We must come again and yet again to our Father to let him love us as Bernard of Clairvaux did, so that passion for God begins to rise up anew and to burn in our hearts. I never used to be able to say, "I love God." But today his love is a burning in my heart that I can no longer extinguish. It is like a greenness of life sprouting up in me, or a well of water that overflows.

Love for Others

It is axiomatic that love for God is accompanied by love for our neighbors. To say "I love God" while failing to be moved by my neighbor's plight is to confess to a false love for God, a love of something other than God. Scougall says, "A soul possessed with divine love must need be enlarged toward all mankind, in a sincere and unbounded affection, because of the relation they have to God, being his creatures, *and having something of his image stamped upon them.*"[11]

Jesus, when he was asked, put the two most important commandments together, saying, " 'Love the Lord your God with all your heart and with all your soul and with all your mind.' This is the first and greatest commandment. And the second is like it: 'Love your neighbor as yourself' " (Mt 22:37-39).

I confess I have a long way to go in this respect. Yes, I do weep, even sob, as I see the devastation of war and its effects on people in Europe and parts of Africa. But there are still people, Christian and non-Christian, whom I resent. The fact that they have "something of his image stamped upon them" makes no difference. I am called to love them, and I don't. Therefore the life of God within me must develop further.

Years ago when I worked as a psychiatrist I would invite some of my patients to the church I attended. Not all of my fellow parishioners were delighted. Perhaps preconceived notions about "mental patients" got in the way. Foolishly, I had not anticipated the difficulty. I loved my patients, and it had never occurred to me that other Christians would not. The image of God—does anyone see it in their neighbors today?

The reaction of my fellow Christians raises important questions in my mind.

Jesus once defined *neighbor* to a lawyer, perhaps a graduate scribe, who seems to have been a stickler for definitions. It is important to read the account of this encounter carefully. Jesus told him the story of the good Samaritan, in which two religious persons (a priest and a Levite) left a badly beaten man lying in the road, whereas a Samaritan paid for him to be cared for. Jesus then asked him a question: "Which of these three do you think was a neighbor to the man who fell into the hands of robbers?" It was a penetrating question. To frame it in idiomatic English, "Who acted like a real neighbor?"

The expert in the law replied, "The one who had mercy on him." And Jesus told him, "Go and do likewise" (Lk 10:25-37).

The so-called legal expert was probably, as I said a moment ago, a scribe who had developed expertise in Torah, the Law of Moses. He was testing the orthodoxy of the Son of God—"witch-hunting," if you like.

First, Jesus affirmed that love of God is accompanied by love of my neighbor. So Jesus passed the first test easily. The lawyer may have anticipated this. To me, he seems at first to have had a patronizing attitude to Jesus. In order to show that the problem was far more complicated than Jesus may have realized, he asked, "Who is my neighbor?" ("It's all very well to say I must love my neighbor. But define *neighbor* for me, please.")

The question had an obvious answer, one that brought conviction to the expert. The Son of God answered with a parable. From the parable we gather that we are to stand ready to help any person in need whom God may bring across our paths. Scougall tells us that the life of God within us, "so far from wronging or injuring any person," will cause us rather to "resent any evil that befalls others, *as if it happened to [ourselves]*" (emphasis mine).

A critical spirit is incompatible with love. It is also incompatible with true spiritual discernment.[12] God, by his Spirit, has for several years now been merciless with me about the matter of critical attitudes toward other people, especially to other Christians. I know that Jesus cursed Pharisees, and I know that pharisaism is widespread among Christians.

But, unlike Jesus, I am not called on to curse pharisaical brothers and sisters. And until my bad habit of criticism is destroyed, I will not be in a position even to talk about pharisaism in the church. To be critical is to be a Pharisee. I am slowly learning not to be a Pharisee.

When I say, "God, by his Spirit, is merciless with me," you must understand that sometimes he has to be merciless to be merciful. Let me put it this way. For several years, the moment I engage in critical thoughts of a fellow Christian—a habit I have long been prone to—at once the Holy Spirit is "on my tail." Slowly I am becoming grateful, for this correction is teaching me both the nature of love and how Christ could so easily mingle with "tax collectors and sinners."

It is true that hearing the gospel itself was the greatest need of the man who was beaten by thieves in Jesus' parable, and sharing the gospel must be an integral part of any cleansing of wounds or giving of money. But love is love. It is not an attempt to improve our evangelistic statistics. We all recognize that love is shown by all we do, not just by preaching. Love is more than evangelistic scalp-hunting. The love with which I minister the gospel is the same love that moves me to do all I can to help someone. There are not two loves in me, but one. Love-for-God-and-neighbor. Once again, love is love. It acts like love acts.

When Jesus read from the Scriptures in the synagogue in Nazareth, he chose the following words from Isaiah 61:

The Spirit of the Lord is on me,
>because he has anointed me
>to preach good news to the poor.
He has sent me to proclaim freedom for the prisoners
>and recovery of sight for the blind,
to release the oppressed,
>to proclaim the year of the Lord's favor. (Lk 4:18-19)

Our understanding of the Great Commission begins at this point. Matthew 28:18-20 must be understood in the context of what the gospel anointing is all about. Good news is particularly for the poor. In all national and widespread revivals, the most prominent feature is the large number of conversions among the poor and uneducated. For the poor constitute our neighbors also.

How do we define *poor?* From Isaiah's words I would see the poor as those who are disadvantaged in and exploited by the rest of society—society's victims. They include prostitutes, drunks, drug addicts, the mentally ill, the hopeless—sinners. Jesus was criticized for eating with these sorts of people. Though their sins are socially and ecclesiastically unacceptable sins, our socially excused sins are no less sin. Under the skin we are the same. God bypasses our strategies of reaching "key people" for Christ. He prefers to glorify his own name as he pours out his Spirit from time to time, awakening men and women of all classes both to the terror of their sin and to the mercy of Christ.

Jesus loved and spent time with sinners. Most churches do not. In this respect churches differ radically from their Lord. Why? Perhaps because we share neither his heart nor his life. We do not understand his anointing. Whatever the reason, Jesus attracted the sort of people that churches fail to attract.

With the passing of winter, the first sign of recovering life in a fruit tree is the appearance of buds and leaves. A dazzling display of blossom soon follows. As the sun's warmth increases, the delicate petals fall, carpeting the ground in white or pink. Then comes the fruit. God can do the same thing, whether with natural blossoms or supernatural. For in gospel terms "fruit" is not soul-winning, or at least not confined to soul-winning, but the fruit of the Spirit, the evidence of the life of God developing within us.

> Aaron's staff . . . had not only sprouted but had budded, blossomed and produced almonds. (Num 17:8)

As we have seen, the most important fruit is love. But spiritual fruit is more than love for God and neighbor.

Purity

So far we have looked at passion for God and love for our neighbor, and now we come to purity. Scougall defines purity as "mastery over the inferior appetites."[13] Whether "inferior appetites" are indeed inferior would be a good question. For Scougall it is a matter of the good being the enemy of the best.

When purity is mentioned, most people's thoughts first fly to sexual purity, then to some specific sexual sin of which they are now or have in the past been guilty. Needless to say, purity involves much more than sex, but we may be right to begin there. In *Eros Redeemed* I pointed out the biblical evidence that sexual sin is the main thrust of Satan's strategy in controlling the human race. C. S. Lewis would seem to agree. He says,

> You can get a large audience together for a strip-tease act—that is, to watch a girl undress on the stage. Now suppose you came to a country where you could fill a theatre by simply bringing a covered plate on to the stage and then slowly lifting the cover so as to let everyone see, just before the lights went out, that it contained a mutton chop or a bit of bacon, would you not think that in that country something had gone wrong with the appetite for food?[14]

Our sex drive is where Satan begins in his attempts to control us.

Purity is a plant of slow growth, and sexual purity, because it involves purity of thought, often grows slowly. As we shall discover in a later chapter of this book, we best attain sexual purity by fanning the flames of the life of God within us.

But purity embraces much, much more. It is best conceived as a certain simplicity, a paring down of all motives to love alone—love of God and love of neighbor. On the path of holiness I soon begin to discover that my love for God and neighbor is largely composed of self-interest. Without realizing what I do, I confuse love with merely trying to please. I aim to make my neighbor like me, approve of me, admire me. I find myself foolishly even thinking of God in the same way. Trying to please is not the same thing as loving. Merely trying to please can be motivated by pure self-interest. I want to be liked. But true love comes from God alone, awakening neighbor love.

Gradually God purifies us. He uses trials. On the rare occasions when my wife gets sick, I begin to discover how thoroughly selfish and unloving I can be. God shows me the extent to which my so-called love is still fairly shallow. If we are ever to win a lost world, trials *must* do their work in us.

I said that purity consists of "a certain simplicity, a paring down of all motives to love alone—love of God and love of neighbor." Let me get back to sex, and confine myself to sexual relations within marriage, in order to illustrate what I mean. How does love differ from lust? When does lust begin?

Let me start with lust. Most people who confess sexual lust to me seem to confuse sexual *feelings* with sexual lust. Sexual feelings are God-created. In themselves they are not evil, but holy. It is only when they take God's place that they become sinful. While the word *holy* and *sex* may seem to belong to different worlds, they do so because Satan's policy all along has been to create an aura of unclean allure about sexuality. Some of us get around this by being playful and using sexual baby talk, others by being clinically detached, and yet others by being crass and crude. All such approaches miss the glory and wonder of sexuality. To "get it right" we need to understand the God-givenness of physical sexual feelings and to discover that love and sex go together. We need to *love* our spouses sexually—that is, not only physically but with our hearts, our whole beings.

Love? Love "is patient and kind." It considers the other person. It does not "use" another person to gratify an appetite. That which is physical (are we not all physical?) combines with that which is spiritual. For we are both, and will always be so. Sexual relations reflect the divine intimacy with God, which we only begin to experience here. Once we are desexed, we will experience that to which sexual intimacy points—we will *know as we are known.*

In the meantime we must begin to learn that simple love for others in relation to all our physical appetites, sexual or otherwise. To crave food or sleep greedily is to worship food or sleep (or the fallen angelic "gods" of food and sleep). It is also, at times, to be unwilling to serve others in our idolatry. We are quite capable of worshiping the ancient gods through the indulgence of our appetites. All our appetites are good and God-created. But sin has lured us into worshiping desire instead of worshiping God. We will know we are beginning to transgress when our physical appetites blind us to the needs and desires of others. At that point we will have stopped worshiping God, the God who loves us all.

Humility

What is humility? Bernard of Clairvaux, borrowing from St. Benedict, describes twelve steps to achieve it. Bernard points to Jesus, telling us to accept the invitation of his yoke, seeing that Jesus himself is "meek and lowly in heart."[15] Christ teaches humility. But you have to walk in step with him for a long time to learn from him.

Humility is the opposite of pride, the first and greatest sin, and the one often associated with a measure of doubt about God's word. Bernard of Clairvaux defines it as "the ability of a person to see himself as he truly is and so discover his own unworthiness."[16] I like the first half of this definition. The last bit is true enough, but it is never the end of the matter. I am indeed unworthy—unworthy of admiration, unworthy of kindness, unworthy of grace, unworthy of love, unworthy even of respect—since I have defaced the image of God that I bear. But the matter must not rest there. Indeed, it is only the beginning. God offers me all the things I am unworthy of. Humility is to know both that though I am thoroughly unworthy, I yet receive kindness, forgiveness and love.

I like Scougall's definition the best. He defines humility as "great deadness toward the glory of the world and the applause of men." Splendid! I want that! This definition "gets" me where it hurts. My value must lie not in other people's opinion of me but in the fact that God loves me.

For God is the kind of person one can love. John Piper says this about him: "God is never irritable or edgy. He is never fatigued or depressed or blue or moody or stressed out. His anger never has a short fuse. He is not easily annoyed."[17] And God even admires me. That is, he admires the "me" he himself is creating within me. As he looks on his handiwork, at the model of me he thought of before time began, a smile crosses his face, and he nods with paternal joy. For he begins to see the image of his Son in me. When that divine smile, and that alone, is the basis of my self-evaluation, my competitiveness goes, my concern about my reputation and my need for other people's approval go. And my peace begins to flow.

Humility is not self-hatred. A humble person is a person who is still and at rest, not (as Andrew Murray would put it) "fretted or sore." A truly humble person is freed from disappointments, able to smile at criticism. To be humble is to be perpetually hidden in God's presence while being outwardly in the midst of tumult. It is the peace of knowing that whatever criticism or bitterness is leveled at me, I am safe in my strong tower, loved and forgiven. It is neither the squirming obsequiousness of Uriah Heep nor a feeling of inferiority, and certainly it is not self-hate or self-loathing. Self-hate and self-loathing are pride gone wrong.

Lewis's essay on pride is well known and includes many comments on humility. It was this essay, you will recall, that turned Charles Colson's life from a quest for political prominence and worldly success to a devotion to Christ's kingdom. Here are Lewis's words again:

Do not imagine that if you meet a really humble person he will be what most people call "humble" nowadays. . . . Probably all you will think about him is that he seemed a cheerful, intelligent chap who took a real interest in what *you* said to *him*. . . . He will not be thinking about humility: he will not be thinking about himself at all.[18]

"Not thinking about himself at all." Some of us have to let that life within us develop further!

The Fruit of the Spirit

Fruit is the product of life. Once again, in Scripture the notion of fruitfulness does not refer primarily to soul-winning, but to a godly character. When Scougall says that the life of God is characterized by "love to God, charity to man, purity and humility," he is listing some of what Paul has called "the fruit of the Spirit." A tree's *life* will produce *fruit*.

"But the fruit of the Spirit is love, joy, peace, patience, kindness, goodness, faithfulness, gentleness and self-control. Against such things there is no law" (Gal 5:22-23). You notice that Paul does not speak of the fruits (plural) of the Spirit, but the *fruit*. The fruit of the Spirit is a character that exemplifies certain qualities, several of which Paul mentions. When you share God's life, you begin to share his character. Jesus himself lists a few in Matthew 5—poverty of spirit (v. 3), mourning (v. 4), meekness (v. 5), a craving for righteousness (v. 6), mercy (v. 7), purity (v. 8), a tendency to promote peace (v. 9) yet also to get yourself persecuted (v. 10).

We could go on forever discussing the qualities of sanctification, but to do so is a waste of time. It gets our eyes on ourselves and on performance—our performance—rather than on Christ. All we need to know is that we can expect to see such qualities popping up in our own lives and the lives of people in whom the Holy Spirit is working. It does no harm to examine ourselves from time to time, but our focus must not be on the qualities themselves but on the divine life that gives rise to them. The qualities spring from life, from its development. We are powerless to produce them, and trying to do so is a waste of time.

Focusing on your pride will never make you humble. Instead of worrying about your bad temper, focus your mind on how kind God is to dwell inside you. Your bad temper will melt in proportion to the time you spend thanking God for his moment-by-moment indwelling. It is his love for you that matters infinitely more than your love for him. I hope I have already made this clear. Your love springs from his, from being loved.

Read the last part of Romans 8. Paul seems to be saying that there is nothing, *absolutely* nothing, that can separate us from the love of God in Christ.

The Invasion
The Holy Spirit inhabits our spirits. Our spirits are the gateway to our sinful bodies, which are by rights the Spirit's temple. Thus the Spirit of the Father and the Spirit of the Son, in the person of the Holy Spirit, invade our bodies, penetrating its very cells.

I wonder if we grasp the significance of this. Sin dwells in our physical bodies. Sin comes to us through the seed of our parents. And the seed of our parents bears with it not only their own sins but also all the sins of the thousands of generations that preceded them. How this works out in vulnerability to specific sins is unique to each of us. Your ancestry almost certainly includes a smattering of thieves, murderers, pimps, whores, homosexuals, slave dealers, witches and pirates. All of them have contributed to the DNA and RNA that you are made of.

A children's nursery rhyme tells us that little boys are made of "slugs and snails and puppy dogs' tails." The reality is both infinitely better and infinitely worse—more glorious and more ghastly. It is worse because we bear the seed of the greatest rogues the earth has ever produced. We will pass that seed on to any children we may sire or bear—with whatever we have added. But the reality is also better than "puppy dogs' tails." It is better because we were created initially to bear God's image. That image has been defaced, but it can be restored. Indeed, that is what the invasion of our bodies is all about.

The Pursuit of Holiness

During recent decades, physicians and surgeons have become increasingly aware of the importance of studying health as well as disease. Many now believe that disease correction begins with disease prevention. The current trend is to study and promote health, so as to forestall some of the enormous expense and effort involved in combating disease. In this chapter I have striven to argue a similar emphasis in relation to spiritual life and health. We combat sin best of all by fanning the flames of life.

Perhaps I alarmed you by quoting and then describing Scougall's criteria for the presence of divine life. If so, I am not sorry. We live in days when Christians need to be aroused from slumber. Someone may even have asked themselves, *Do I have* any *divine life?* If that should be the question in your mind, let me bring reassurance to you.

If the question troubles you, then know this: First, you could not be anxious about your soul unless God had not first awakened you. And second, God never awakens you to your true condition unless he has already chosen you to belong to him. Not infrequently these days I come across members of evangelical churches who suddenly are awakened to the fact that they have never been Christians and that they do not have the life of God in their souls. They had gone through some sort of process by which they were encouraged to receive Jesus, without understanding what "receiving Jesus" involved. Consequently, though they went through a kind of conversion experience, it was not a regenerating experience, the kind that brings the life of God.

John the apostle uses the expression "receive [Jesus]" at the start of his Gospel. The context is important. John is discussing the arrival of God the Son on the planet—which, like the rest of the universe, he himself had created. It belonged to him. He had come to reclaim it and its peoples.

He was in the world, and though the world was made through him, the world did not recognize him. He came to that which was his own, but his own did not receive him. Yet to all who received him, to those who believed in his name, he gave the right to become children of God—children born not of natural descent, nor of human decision or a husband's will, but born of God. (Jn 1:10-13)

Though the world as a whole failed to recognize Jesus, a number of people did. They recognized him *as their rightful Lord*. You cannot receive Christ in any other way. He who is Savior is likewise Lord. He is not two persons, but one.

In the same way, God's child has God's life and God's person within his or her body. This is where we began. If you are a Christian, you have divine life inside your body. Sanctification consists of focusing more on promoting that life than on fighting sin.

Are the embers covered with ash? Fan them into flame! The life itself combats the sin. So fan the flames, and add more of the fuel of Scripture truth. Or, to change the metaphor, water the plant! Get it into the sun, and make sure it has soil to grow in!

As you do these things a new ardor of love will eventually begin to burn within you. You will begin to "see" the Lord.

11

GAZING ON CHRIST

And we all, with unveiled face, beholding the glory of the Lord,
are being changed into his likeness from one degree
of glory to another; for this comes from the Lord who is the Spirit.
(2 Corinthians 3:18 RSV)

*I*N THE PREVIOUS CHAPTER I SAID THAT THE MOST IMPORTANT WAY TO RE-duce the "disease" of sin in your life is to nourish the divine life that is already there. If you do that, a progressive transformation begins—of you, your personality, your character—as the verse at the head of this chapter tells us.

Progressive Transformation

In 2 Corinthians 3:18 the transformation is described as a progression in glory—"from one degree of glory to another." Paul tells us we "are being transformed into [the Lord's] likeness with ever-increasing glory, which comes from the Lord who is the Spirit."

Ever-increasing *what?* Glory? What does glory have to do with the average Christian? Surely our business is to avoid personal glory. C. S. Lewis had similar qualms:

> Glory suggests two ideas to me, one of which seems wicked and the other ridiculous. Either glory means to me fame, or it means luminosity. As for the first, since to be famous means to be better known than other people, the desire for fame appears to me as a competitive passion and therefore of hell rather than heaven. As for the second, who wishes to become a kind of living electric light bulb?[1]

But Lewis goes on to tell how as he read more widely, he discovered that Christians as different as John Milton, Samuel Johnson and Thomas Aquinas all seemed to take *glory* in the first sense of desiring fame and reputation.

In England we used to sing a hymn that I came to despise. The chorus began,

Oh that will be glory for me,

Glory for me, glory for me . . .[2]

Glory for me? *How despicable! How self-centered,* I thought. *Christ is to be glorified, not me!* Like a Pharisee, I felt nothing but abhorrence and contempt for the notion of "glory for me." But I had underestimated the love and the self-giving of Christ. Jesus wants to be glorified *in us*—in his people (Jn 17:10). He himself is the revelation of God's glory. "The Son is the radiance of God's glory and the exact representation of his being" (Heb 1:3). In his amazing goodness Christ wishes to impart that glory to us, and to begin here and now.

He wants to glorify you, to be glorified in and through you. He wants the world to see his glory shining through you in this life. People may not see your face shining as Moses' face shone, but they should perceive something in both your countenance and your behavior that speaks to them of God's glory.

The chorus of the hymn I so despised ends as follows:

When by his grace I shall look on his face,

That will be glory, be glory for me!

The words of the hymn are about heaven, about what happens after we die. They refer to a future when we shall all see Christ no longer "through a glass darkly," but face to face.

Yet the verse that heads this chapter does not hold up only a future hope. It deals with the present, seeming to say something much more awesome than the hymn. It claims that as we gaze on Jesus in this present life, the transformation will begin. Glory comes to us as we give ourselves to beholding him. In the degree that the life of God grows in the soul of saved sinners, the glory shines brighter. We change as we gaze. Angels observe the radiance, while our fellow humans catch a glimpse of a change in our attitude and manner.

Sliding into Glory

In my mind glory is closely allied to beauty. I love beauty—cool forests with their damp greenness filled with bird song, the ravishing glory of headlands overlooking the glittering blue sea, the howling of wind, the tinkling of a stream in a dell, the crash of waves on a beach, even the satisfying roar of thunder, or of a waterfall. I also enjoy the way human beings can capture creation's beauty in paint, statue and music. And believe it or not, there are mathematical beauties (a friend of mine studying "pure" math told me enthusiastically of a "simply beautiful equation"—there was no other way he could express it).

Glory and beauty are related. The glory of God is revealed in all the forms of beauty I have mentioned and many more. The highest beauty of all is moral and ethical—a beauty that reaches its climax in the person of God himself. Among other things, God's glory—his ethical beauty—reveals itself in the fires of his holy and utterly unselfish love.

But what is our relation to the beauty of God's character? The answer to this question is tied up in a translation problem in 2 Corinthians 3:18. The New International Version reads, "And we, who with unveiled faces all reflect the Lord's glory, are being transformed into his likeness with ever-increasing glory, which comes from the Lord, who is the Spirit." Compare this to the Revised Standard Version reading, which appears at the head of the chapter. It says we *behold* the glory, whereas the NIV translation says we *reflect* it (but adds the word *contemplate* as a footnote alternative).

Which is correct—reflect, behold or contemplate? Is it important? It matters a whole lot, and unlike the NIV (which I usually quote) I opt for the "behold/contemplate" reading. How could you be transformed into a glory without having beheld it?

If you gaze at or think a great deal about someone you like, you tend to copy them unwittingly. In that sense, but in that sense only, you "reflect" them. You do not reflect them as a mirror reflects, though Paul is using a "mirror" word here—*katoptrizomai*. But more on the translation issues later.

Henry Scougall, the young professor who died at the age of twenty-eight, comments on the fact that we imitate those we love: "The images of these do frequently present themselves unto the mind, and by a secret force and energy insinuate into the very constitution of the soul, and mould and fashion it into their own likeness."[3] He even points out that the process is automatic and *unconscious*. You don't have to sweat it. "Hence we may see how easily lovers and friends do slide into the imitations of those whom they affect [or love]; and how, even before they are aware, they begin to resemble them."[4] In other words, people "slide into" Christlikeness, "even before they are aware" of doing so.

You say, "I thought you once wrote a book called *The Fight*. Why are you now talking about the Christian life as though it were effortless?"

The area of struggle, the area in which the Christian life becomes a fight, a bitter "fight to the death," is the area of faith. It is by faith that we experience transformation—a faith by which we are mostly unconscious of the glory that is coming to us. I know I said in the previous chapter that faith is a gift, that it is imparted to us. But once it is given, it must be used. It is not elastic, but like a muscle it must be exercised, at times grimly. It will be a fight even to find time to gaze on Christ.

On the Other Side of the Mirror

But we all, with open face beholding as in a glass the glory of the Lord, are changed into the same image from glory to glory, even as by the Spirit of the Lord. (2 Cor 3:18 KJV)

The protagonist of the second story I wrote in the Archives of Anthropos series was Mary, a fat and pimply girl who longed to be beautiful. A witch offered her certain crystals, promising that if she swallowed them she would be transformed—beautiful for an hour the first day, all day the second and permanently on the third. The changes in her body would feel rather uncomfortable, and she would know her beauty was fading when the discomfort began to pass. The witch also gave her a magic mirror in which she could see herself. But Mary was warned that on the first day she must not continue to look into the mirror any longer than an hour. She would know by her body's feelings when the hour was up.

Mary ignored the warning. Intrigued by her own beauty and enjoying the fun of making faces at herself, she continued to look even after she knew her beauty was fading. It was then that she discovered that all along there had been another being on the other side of the mirror, expertly mimicking every gesture she made. It was a terrifying discovery. Who or what was that someone on the other side of the mirror?[5]

We make a similar kind of discovery, only in our case not terrifying but wonderful, when we learn the truth of 2 Corinthians 3:18. Paul uses similar language in another passage—1 Corinthians 13:12: "Now we see but a poor reflection as in a mirror; then we shall see face to face. Now I know in part; then I shall know fully, even as I am fully known." *Esoptron*, the word Paul uses here for "mirror," conveys the same image as *katoptrizomai*. Mirrors in Paul's day were bronze. Bronze mirrors are still used today—for example, on elevator doors in some hotels. The modern version gives a pretty decent reflection, but it is not perfect. And it is to such a mirror we are invited—to see someone beyond the mirror. Of course part of the difficulty is in our seeing. We perceive Christ only dimly as we read about him in Scripture and meditate on what we read. How greatly we yearn to see him more clearly! Some days we do not see him at all. He comes in this sense when he chooses.

We are not in control. There is a drawing near of Christ, a mysterious operation of the Spirit, that is his prerogative alone. We must know our helplessness and be in submission to his prerogatives. As time passes, we are increasingly able to apprehend him by faith. True to his promise, he draws near as we do. Yet there is nothing we can do to create that sense of mysterious nearness. We know it when it happens, and when it does so we begin to be changed.

In one sense, of course, the Lord is always near us, never leaving us. But at times he can make us much more vividly aware of him. At times too we unwittingly pull away from him—then wrongly suppose it is he who has pulled away. We learn about the mystery of his being little by little. So let us draw near "with a sincere heart, in full assurance of faith" (Heb 10:22).

We are to look at Christ, who awaits us beyond a mirror. And viewing him thus, we will be transformed progressively into his image. Instead of that image reflecting us, we will begin gradually to "reflect" the image behind the mirror. Yet I put quotation marks around the word *reflect* for a reason. We do not reflect as a mirror reflects. We are actually being changed. Christ's glory can gradually become ours. There is no difficulty about the translation if we understand this.

What does it feel like to be shining with glory? I think I know, but I cannot be sure. In *Eros Redeemed* I described how one early morning I hurried through the routine of showering and flung a bathrobe around me to meet with the Lord in my study. As I began to reflect on his presence and kindness, deep into my spirit the Holy Spirit spoke the words "Take off your bathrobe and stand before me naked."

I did what I was told, feeling ridiculous. I became conscious of the Lord's eyes surveying me from head to toe. I never saw either his person or his eyes, but I knew what was happening. The thing that took me completely by surprise was that *I was then no longer naked!* I was unclothed, but not naked. There was a shining forth of a glory, Christ's glory, that I could not see.

You see, I believe we'll all be unclothed in heaven. "How ridiculous!" you say. "My Bible tells me we will be robed in white linen." Yes, but it tells us that the white linen is "the righteousness of the saints." " 'Fine linen, bright and clean, was given her to wear.' (Fine linen stands for the righteous acts of the saints)" (Rev 19:8).

Our righteousness is not ours. Even when we do perform righteous acts, we can take no credit for them, for we are servants of the Most High (Lk 17:10). Therein lies our glory! You were chosen before the earth began not to display yourself, but to display God's glory (Eph 1:11-12). That glory invaded your being when you entered into a relationship with Jesus Christ.

The gospel is the gospel of the glory of Christ, who is the *eikōn* or image of the living God (2 Cor 4:4). And the more you gaze on him with admiration, the more you will become like him, bearing that glory.

Degrees of Glory

Already we have seen three things about this transformation. First, it can begin in this life—that is, here and now. It is a present transformation. Second, it is a glorious transformation, glory imparted to the believer. Finally, it is progressive. It proceeds from "one degree of glory to another," as one translation puts it, or "from glory to glory," in the words of another translation. Present, progressive and glorious. But 2 Corinthians 3:18 tells us more.

1. It is passive.

2. It concerns the permanent nature of our service.

3. It is brought about by the Holy Spirit.

Passive? All the translations seem to agree here. They may disagree about the mirroring, but they are united regarding the passive nature of our transformation. We are acted upon. We are not the actors. We "are being transformed" (NRSV, NIV) and "are changed" (KJV). The verbs are in the passive form. They speak of a transformation brought about by the action of God's Spirit, or, if you like, by Christ's glorious life being manifested within us.

I hate passivity, and always tend to resist the passivity in my own nature. But the process being described by Paul is passive only in one sense—that God initiates it. It does call for our response to what God does, and we must make that response.

We collaborate with him by gazing upon him. Already I have pointed out that we do in fact fan the flames, throw more fuel on the fire and so on. We feed the life. Therefore it is very important that we understand 2 Corinthians 3:18 properly. If the Holy Spirit is to do his work, we have to be doing the right thing, whether gazing on Christ or reflecting him. What we can be sure of is that as we gaze as we are supposed to, all will be well, and the process of our transformation will continue.

At its heart, the change in us has to do with ongoing repentance. You will remember that in the chapter on repentance I pointed out that God initiates it and that we respond to what the Holy Spirit is showing us. As we spend time in Christ's presence, contemplating his beauty, it is as though more light begins to fall on the ugliness of our sin, and at the same time on the grace and exceeding kindness of God. God is changing me personally day after day through this process. In some mysterious manner it is as though he begins to dig at the roots of sins that, like weeds, have cropped up repeatedly in my life. As he pulls them up by the roots, they are gone!

The only problem is that there are always more sins that I had never even thought of. The process is endless, and this can be discouraging. But the fact is, I am in a long process of change. The change is from one degree of glory to another. Over years Christ has gone over my financial life, my sex life, my relationships with family members, fellow Christians and unbelievers. As I collaborate with him in what he is doing, I change. But the operation seems everlasting. It never stops.

Gazing on Christ

When I advise people to gaze on the glory of Christ, a distressed look often comes on their faces. They say, "Yeah—but . . ." Frequently they say nothing more. How do you gaze on Christ—on his glory? What do the words mean—if they mean anything at all? In *Knowing God* J. I. Packer reminds us of something most of us have forgotten: the important role that meditation has in the life of the Christian.

> Meditation is the activity of calling to mind, and thinking over, and dwelling on, and applying to oneself, the various things that one knows about the works and ways and purposes and promises of God. It is an activity of holy thought, consciously performed in the presence of God, under the eye of God, by the help of God, as a means of communion with God.[6]

This is how I would like to define gazing on Christ, the real Messiah, Jesus, who manifests the real God. "Gazing" means to hang on his every word, as Mary did when she sat at Jesus' feet. It means to meditate on his words and on all we learn about him in the Gospels and epistles. All this we do in the Spirit's quickening presence. When we do that, "in the presence of God, under the eye of God, by the help of God, as a means of communion with God," something very significant can happen to us. A veil is removed from our eyes, as meditation slips into contemplation. We see what for many is invisible. The glories of Christ can be displayed before our wondering eyes.

The thesis makes sense. As Scougall pointed out, the more you admire someone, the more you tend to become like them. I remember my near-adoration of Martyn Lloyd-Jones during my student days. I was overwhelmed by his teaching—whatever I could get of it, for he never wrote books, at least in those days. "I am a preacher," he would say, in answers to questions about why he didn't write.

Many people, particularly pastors and ministers, shared my admiration of Lloyd-Jones. Some of them shared neither his spirit nor his essential genius, yet even they became a sort of caricature of him. They grew into little Lloyd-Joneses, expounding the letter of Scripture in sonorous, academic, nasalized tones, with just a hint of a Welsh accent.

They lacked Lloyd-Jones's spirit. For God had done something in the man that eluded those who never saw his heart. Yet notice what had happened: they had become like what they saw in the great man. Some may even have compared in intellect with him, though they were surely few. But they missed the secret of his heart. He had gazed on glory.

It is the same with gazing at Christ and admiring him. We do not want his merely superficial characteristics. His cloak and tunic would serve us ill. We must not become caricatures. We must crave the glory that is at his heart. And this is what he wants for us, character transformation. Lewis says that what we really crave is "to please God . . . to be a real ingredient in the divine happiness . . . to be loved by God, not merely pitied, but delighted in as an artist delights in his work or a father in a son—it seems impossible, a weight or burden of glory which our thoughts can hardly sustain. But so it is."[7]

The Translation Issue

Think back to the verse at the head the chapter about gazing on Christ. As I pointed out, one of the key words in the NIV translation is the word *reflect*: with unveiled faces we "reflect" Christ's glory. The RSV reads "beholding." In the King James Version, too, the basic idea is clear. Occasionally the old version is the best of all! The NRSV sticks with the RSV and the King James. The Revised English Bible and the New American Bible agree, while the Jerusalem Bible opts for "reflect."

Like me, John Piper prefers the translation "beholding." In an explanatory note referring to the verse he says, "The Greek word translated 'beholding' (*katoptrizomenoi*) can mean 'reflecting' and some interpreters take it to mean that here. . . . But the preceding and following contexts lead me to think 'beholding' is correct."[8]

We do not merely reflect the glory of Christ, we share it. It shines from within us. And when we take 2 Corinthians 3:18 as a whole, we see that the key concept is *change*. Isn't that, after all, what the sanctifying process is all about—a changed character in which the glory of Christ can be observed?

A mirror is not changed by what it reflects! Once the image it reflects is removed, the mirror remains a mirror, reflecting anything that comes along. We, in contrast, are to be changed. The change is to be a real change, for only a real change can deliver us from becoming artificial.

"How are you?" Someone smilingly offers a handshake as we walk into church.

"Fine, thank you, and you?"

"Oh, great! Really great!"

We may even have succeeded in convincing ourselves (temporarily, anyway) that we speak truth. Or we may be blind enough to be living in an unreal world. But our greetings as we go in and out of church are largely polite lies. It would ruffle the general pleasantness too much if it were otherwise. No one wants to greet a grouch. We fear the rejection of God's people enough to keep our problems under wraps.

We were redeemed for greater ends. We are to be transformed at the core of our characters. Nothing less will do.

Playing with Mirrors

Let me not hide my sin. You may remember that in the previous chapter I confessed that I need to grow in humility (a sign of the life of God that Scougall talked about). The life of God within me has a ways to go before I am as humble as I ought to be. At this stage I can only try not to give way to the pride within me—to keep pride from having its head.

It so happens that as I type this I am fuming. Rage boils up inside me, basically because I am proud. I struggle against it.

Some years ago the Holy Spirit spoke to me, telling me to drop the title "Doctor." Years before, I had been elated when I had walked for the first time on the wards of a teaching hospital wearing a long white coat instead of a short one. I was now *a doctor!* Later I gained further honors, so that I wound up on the faculty of a medical school. Oh, the unconscious pride, the quiet acceptance of a superiority that belonged more to the role I played than to my real self. The real me was a sinner to whom grace had come!

Yet despite my struggles, I truly am being transformed. I am certainly more holy than I used to be. The fact that I still have a long way to go is not the most important thing. What is important, according to 2 Corinthians 3:18, is that I have begun to behold Christ's image.

The Context of Transformation

A good rule in interpreting a verse of Scripture is to note the context in which it is found. In 2 Corinthians 3—4 Paul is discussing the glory of the ministry committed to him. This is the context in which he talks about our transformation. To preach the gospel is to proclaim the new covenant God has made with us all. In 3:7-8 Paul asks, "Now if the ministry that brought death, which was engraved in letters on stone, came with glory, so that the Israelites could not look steadily at the face of Moses because of its glory, fading though it was, will not the ministry of the Spirit be even more glorious?"

He then goes on to tell the story of how when Moses came down from Mount Sinai the second time, carrying the stone tablets of God's law, his face shone with radiance. The Israelites who saw him were astonished and asked, in essence, "What has happened to Moses? Why is his face shining like that?"

Moses had asked God to show him the divine glory, and though he had not been permitted to see God's face, so to speak, he had experienced a close encounter with some aspect of God. Now, you cannot get that close to God without being changed. Something about the energy of the divine being changes you. And Moses was changed. He shone with divine glory. What is more, *God* allowed the Israelites to see this glory, something that under normal circumstances is hidden from mortals. I am not surprised that the Israelites were scared when they saw Moses. "When Moses came down from Mount Sinai with the two tablets of the Testimony in his hands, he was not aware that his face was radiant because he had spoken with the LORD. When Aaron and all the Israelites saw Moses, his face was radiant, and they were afraid to come near him" (Ex 34:29-30).

The glory on Moses' face was like the glory of Christ on the Mount of Transfiguration. The transfiguration opened the apostles' eyes to enable them to see something that had been there all along—messianic glory. The Son of God had become the suffering servant. It had been essential that his glory remain hidden, but on the mountain Peter, James and John were enabled to see beyond the veil of time and space, to perceive other spiritual beings and to see a glory that was really there. In the same way, in Moses' day, God was letting the Israelites see the transformation in a man who had experienced a close encounter with God.

It still happens occasionally. During a revival in the Hebrides in the 1940s, one woman saw that same shining on the face of a child.

In Moses' case the glory was a fading glory. It didn't last. Gradually, as the effects of his encounter with God wore off, the radiance dimmed. Moses covered his face, and some commentators suggest that he did so to conceal the fading. Yet the radiance was renewed repeatedly each time he went back into God's presence.

Paul cites this fading of divine glory in order to compare the old and new covenants. Under the new covenant Christ has done something, he tells us, that produces a glory that does not need to fade. "If what was fading away came with glory, how much greater is the glory of that which lasts!" (2 Cor 3:11).

How Does Glory Feel?

What is the deepest longing in your heart? Do you know? Most people do not. I know what I want—approval, the approval that matters most of all, divine approval.

Three-year-olds are different from adults. They want approval, too, and our approval will do. Praise a child and watch her glow. There is no visible glow, to be sure, but the way her eyes light up tells you something. And you, like the rest of us, need the same thing.

The same thing? I sought human accolades for years—even though they made me uncomfortable. I lived (and I am still tempted to live) for the praise of others, just as the Israelites hankered for leeks and garlic. The only trouble with commendations, leeks and garlic is that none of these earth products satisfy. Each new accomplishment and the affirming words that accompany it immediately prove stale, so that we crave more and must aim at ever greater achievements.

Imagine having all the fame in the world, the approval of multitudes. Jesus had it once—as he rode on the foal of an ass into Jerusalem—and how long did it last? Not only does human praise never satisfy, it never endures.

So what is it we want most? We long for the divine, the eternal "Well done!"

Remember I said that Lewis was surprised to find that Milton, Johnson and Aquinas all seemed to take *glory* in the "wrong" sense of the word. Read how Lewis clarifies what he began to see about the wisdom of Aquinas, Milton and Johnson regarding fame: "But not fame conferred by our fellow creatures—fame with God, approval or (I might say) 'appreciation' by God. And then, when I had thought it over, I saw that this view was scriptural; nothing can eliminate from the parable the divine accolade, 'well done, thou good and faithful servant.' "[9]

Lewis recommends the attitude of a child, reminding us that "perfect humility dispenses with modesty."[10] In every human heart there is a longing that out of a mistaken modesty we will not acknowledge. It is the longing Satan had, and for this reason we mistakenly reject it. For Satan wanted it *in competition with God and in rebellion against him*. He wanted what no created being may have: more glory than God himself. God had already loaded him with glory.

And God wants to do the same for his human sons and daughters—and *this* is exactly what we want. As Lewis puts it, "We do not merely want to *see* beauty, though, God knows, even that is bounty enough. We want something else which can hardly be put into words—to be united with the beauty we see, to pass into it, to receive it into ourselves, to bathe in it, to become part of it."[11]

I believe that in God's sight you may already be shining with a glory he has been giving you; but instead of being grateful for his kindness, you are too busy looking at your own faults even to be aware of what God has done. It is time you gave him thanks, for he wants to increase that shining, making it ready for the day in which it will be revealed.

12

THE
PASSIONATE
PEOPLE

But you are a chosen people, a royal priesthood,
a holy nation, a people belonging to God, that you may declare
the praises of him who called you out of darkness
into his wonderful light. (1 Peter 2:9)

*S*O FAR I HAVE BEEN WRITING AS THOUGH HOLINESS WERE AN INDIVIDUAL, personal matter. Most books about holiness are addressed to individuals—to isolated soldiers in the army. Scripture, on the other hand, focuses on the corporate aspects of holiness. It has a profound concern with the body of Christ as a whole.

To the early Reformers, the church was just that—a body. For them it was the continuation of what God began doing in Israel. God's words to Israel through Moses were "You will be for me a kingdom of priests and a holy nation" (Ex 19:6). A kingdom is a corporate body.

At the point in ecclesiastical history when Israel turns to the Messiah, the church will have become one, will be as holy as our humanity permits us to be—and a bride Christ will be delighted to come for.

The Bride
Bridegrooms and brides have bodies. The bodily, physical side of love may predominate in the early stages of the marriage, but if things go well the passion, the fire, will extend to every area of the partners' lives. The passionate drives that brought the marriage together will pervade the whole of their beings. You will see it in the expression that changes and softens their faces when their eyes chance to rest on their lover.

Passion begins with the body. It may extend to the rest of the personality, but unless physical attraction is present, unless hand reaches out for hand, or yearns to caress a lock of hair, passion is lacking. And passion is an essential ingredient of a true marriage. Passionate love may breed passionate jealousy, but it will flow out again to the unfaithful lover when that one turns again in shame and sorrow for what he or she has done. Passionate love that once seemed dead then springs into new life.

In Scripture, Yahweh is a *passionate* lover. Just as a passionate lover loves the children of his marriage with equal passion, Jesus reveals the heart of the triune God when he cries, "O Jerusalem, Jerusalem, you who kill the prophets and stone those sent to you, how often I have longed to gather your children together, as a hen gathers her chicks under her wings, but you were not willing!" (Lk 13:34).

God, though jealous with a great jealousy when his people are unfaithful, offers his love to us when we who are unfaithful lovers turn in true and deep repentance toward him. But he wants passionate love from us. No other love will serve.

Consider a marriage in which one partner lacks passion—whether in the marriage bed or in day-to-day living. First we must realize that the other partner, the passionate one, is very aware of the lack of passion in his or her spouse. Passion demands responding passion and is keenly aware when it is absent. Those spouses who lack passion, however, are often totally unaware, just as people blind from birth lack any conception of color.

How does the passionate partner react to the lack of passion? Hope rises: surely the very ardor of their love will awaken passion in their lover! But eventually one of two things will happen. Either they will turn elsewhere to find the response they crave, or they will quietly despair and cease to hope. They will remain faithful but protect themselves from the pain of unrequited passion.

But God is not like us in this way. In Christ's letter to the Ephesian church, as revealed to the apostle John, we read of a burning passion that *demands* a response. I like Eugene Peterson's powerful rendering of the commendations with which the letter begins: "I see what you've done, your hard, hard work, your refusal to quit. I know you can't stomach evil. . . . I know your persistence, your courage in my cause, that you never wear out. Yet I hold this against you . . ." (Rev 2:2-4 TM). To me this is amazing. Here is a church that works like crazy, that never gives up, that is discerning about evil and takes action on what it discerns, that has unending courage. What more does Christ want?

You will never understand this letter unless you are a passionate lover yourself. Passion calls for passion and will not be content until it gets passion in return.

Picture in your mind a passionate woman. She has room for only one passion in her life—her own husband. But her eyes are haunted. When you find out what the trouble is, you say, "But you have a *wonderful* husband! He works like a slave. He's absolutely tireless. Look how attentive he is to you! He never loses his temper. He's absolutely faithful to you. What more do you want?"

She shrugs her shoulders and turns away with a sigh. She burns, not with lust but with true ardor. And she knows that, attentive and faithful as her husband may be, no similar eagerness burns in him. You can't fake fervor. Only true ardor will do. And the passionate lover cannot stop wanting it.

God is not a sinful human being. He will therefore not turn to another, more satisfactory lover. Nor will he despair. The Ephesian church is one of seven. It is the whole church that Christ loves passionately, and while there is more than a hint that he is quite prepared to give up this one church, he will never give up the whole body of the church in Asia Minor. He complains to the Ephesian church, "But you walked away from your first love. Why? . . . Do you have any idea how far you've fallen? A Lucifer fall!" (Rev 2:4-5 TM).

Again I shake my head. Christ clearly appreciates the Ephesians' very hard work, courage and relentless persistence, yet he is not satisfied. Passion demands passion. Christ demands a passionate response to his passionate love. Nothing less will do. He knows the ardor was there when the church began. It should have been a growing ardor. Instead of that it has cooled. It no longer burns. In the language of *The Message*, he sees the fall from passion as "a Lucifer fall." And every other version, while not naming Lucifer, indicates that the fall was very great. Consider the NIV: "Remember the height from which you have fallen! Repent and do the things you did at first. If you do not repent, I will come to you and remove your lampstand from its place. But you have this in your favor: You hate the practices of the Nicolaitans, which I also hate" (Rev 2:5-6).

The church has fallen from fervor. Christ will not put up with it. He wants a fervent people. When he addresses the Laodicean church in the seventh letter, he is so upset by its lack of passion that he tells these believers that he wants to "spit you out of my mouth" (Rev 3:16). *God hates it when the flames of our passion for him die away while his own burning love cannot.* He will not continue to bear the pain of it.

Judgments and Rewards

Perhaps we are blinded by our mythologies. There is, for instance, the myth of a judgment-free church—a church that will not be judged. We fully understand, to be sure, that "judgment begins in the house of God" (see 1 Pet 4:17). We nod our heads at one another, agreeing. Other churches need judgment. They will get their deserts sooner or later. But not our church. Our church has always been OK, thank you! We have correct doctrine.

But do you have passion?

Of the seven Asia Minor churches addressed in Revelation, only two escaped judgment. God visited the church in judgment, punishing his people as needed. For example, God was at the point of a summary dealing with the church in Thyatira that tolerated Jezebel (a heretical sect that advocated sexual immorality): "I have given her time to repent of her immorality, but she is unwilling. So I will cast her on a bed of suffering, and I will make those who commit adultery with her suffer intensely, unless they repent of her ways" (Rev 2:21-22).

But what happened to the two churches over which no judgment hung? As is commonly the way of things, those two had to endure bitter opposition. Yet their individual fates differed profoundly. Philadelphia was to have "an open door that no one can shut" (3:8) as its members preached the gospel. Better still, their enemies would eventually come and lick their boots—well, sort of. "I will make those who are of the synagogue of Satan, who claim to be Jews though they are not, but are liars—I will make them come and fall down at your feet and acknowledge that I have loved you" (Rev 3:9).

Smyrna, on the other hand, was given the most exalted privilege of all—prolonged opposition, imprisonment and death. The Smyrnans loved Christ with a burning, flaming passion. For them there was to be the highest and most glorious reward of all, the reward of those who are utterly, utterly faithful—that of sharing Christ's personal sufferings.

Do we, in our local churches, love with enough passion to face imprisonment or death? If we don't, then we have fallen far and deep. "Do not be afraid of what you are about to suffer. I tell you, the devil will put some of you in prison to test you, and you will suffer persecution for ten days. Be faithful, even to the point of death, and I will give you the crown of life" (Rev 2:10).

Today martyrdom is beginning again. I remember praying for a man once and in the middle of the prayer being interrupted by the Holy Spirit, who told me "This man will die as a martyr for me!" Horrified, I ended the prayer lamely, not daring to tell him.

The next day, another man who prayed for him burst into tears in the middle of his prayer.

"What was the matter with you when you were praying just now?" I asked him later.

"God told me he is to be a martyr!" he replied.

Martyrdom has never really ceased. It results only from a passionate love for Christ. Lesser loves will go along with some form of compromise. Again and again churches (as with the opposition of certain churches to the Nazi Party in Germany during World War II) have been divided over who comes first in their loyalty. Our salvation may not be in question when we make compromises in our loyalties, but our ardor is.

In a number of areas of the world today Christians suffer persecution to the point of being put to death for their faith. From one area of northern Sudan come reports of crucifixions. In the Muslim world and in the People's Republic of China the persecution can be terrible. Are our love and our faith of a quality to endure such things? We may never face them, but the passion is still demanded.

Denominationalism and Repentance

Another myth I want to mention is similar to the previous one, only now I have a larger scale in mind: the denominational level (Greek Orthodox, Roman Catholic, Anglican and the like). The myth is that our church (that is, our denomination) is the *right* one.

Churches are started by God and completed by human beings. They are a mixture of the divine and the human. They go through what you could call evolutionary phases. And while the divine part cannot be corrupted, the human part certainly can be and always will be.

How can a lukewarm denomination become a passionate one? Only when a congregation within that denomination sets itself to fast and pray. And under what circumstances will that happen? It will happen when an individual in that church repents of his or her own lack of passion. Then the living Christ will enter that person. He will awaken so passionate a longing that the person's prayer for the local church will become importunate. For when Christ, on the heels of our repentance, enters our hearts, he inflames us.

At that point anything may happen. Revivals begin when Christ inflames a single heart. But it is best when that person is a leader in the church.

God's Judgment on the Leaders of His People

Ezekiel 34 makes it clear that when judgment falls, it falls most heavily on leaders. Of those to whom much is given, much is required. In Ezekiel's day the rulers were kings, princes, prophets, priests—those who led Israel and Judah. Today God's concern is ministers, pastors, Sunday-school teachers, deacons, elders, rectors, bishops, priests, general secretaries of interdenominational organizations, youth leaders, women leaders and so on.

In Ezekiel 34 the prophet blames the leaders of God's people *for not sharing God's heart*. God's desire is for his people's good, and God blames shepherds for exploiting their privileges to the detriment of the sheep. Yes, the sheep also are to blame. They trample one another's pasture and muddy one another's water. Like pastor, like sheep. Though God is aware of the responsibility of the sheep, his principal anger is directed against the leaders.

Ezekiel 34 reveals God's own heart. He longs for people, especially for *his own* people. It is not that he needs us, but that we need him.

As he sees the deprivation we suffer he yearns for our wholeness and healing with a yearning we cannot even conceive. And his anger is directed toward unfaithful leaders. It was for this reason that Christ so roundly cursed the Pharisees.

Many church leaders, as far as I can see, seem to be of two kinds. First there are those who hide great weariness and inner bankruptcy behind a façade of smiles. They are close to a place of disenchantment and even despair. Others have developed the mysterious capacity to feed off the sheep—to relish power over congregations or organizations and to exploit the position they are in to the impoverishment of their followers. Though they are blind to what they are doing, theirs is a chosen blindness. What they indignantly deny is precisely what they have chosen. They are the shepherds about whom Ezekiel writes.

God has placed on my heart the burden of knowing what is to happen to a number of Christian leaders in Canada. Such judgments may be his plan elsewhere also. Biblical principles would seem to make it so. But I have been told only about Canada, and God's message has to do with repentance—to whom it will be granted and to whom it will not.

I used to take part in an early-morning prayer meeting once a week, attended mostly by men before they went to work. Our prayer focused on intercession for revival across Canada. One morning at such a meeting, about six years before the writing of this book, something frightening happened to me. I was praying and was in mid-prayer, so to speak, maybe in a particularly fine flight of eloquence—or what I might have thought of as spirituality—when suddenly a curtain was torn aside for just a few seconds.

I was so shattered that immediately my own prayer was obliterated, forgotten. I struggled from the armchair I was sitting in and tried to stand. But I never made it. I lifted up my right hand like a traffic policeman commanding someone to stop, and yelled out something like "No, God, *no!* You must not do that! *Stop!*"

Then I sank back, stunned, shaken and trembling. What had I said? Would God forgive me? We are not supposed to talk to God like that—or are there occasions when we are?

In those brief moments I had seen two things. First I had seen the darkness that falls on men and women when they do not let God be God in their lives (Rom 1:21-23). To me this darkness had been only a biblical concept; I understood it, but I had never actually *seen* the darkness itself. To see it in the spirit was terrifying, shattering. The darkness that can come on us is awful beyond words.

At the same time God told me what was to happen to Christian leaders across Canada. To some repentance would be granted. They would see their sins as God sees them, but also see the redemptive love of Christ for them. Many would weep.

Others would go to their graves unrepentant. If they were truly regenerate they will go to glory, saved by the skin of their teeth. If they are not, then they would still be hellbound. Mercifully, God never told me who was who.

Do you wonder that I yelled out loud? When God's Spirit falls on you to reveal such things, *you would not wish your worst enemy the fate that you know is to be theirs.*

I no longer feel the fear I knew in that moment, though when I think about the vision I am still disturbed. That is not itself my burden. My burden is to keep announcing what I have seen. Some will pay heed, others will mock, still others will ignore me.

Remember, you can't make yourself passionate. Only Christ can awaken passion in you. And to do so he must first enter, then have full possession of your heart. When that happens, you will love him with a burning and unbearable passion.

The Terrible Effects of Spiritual Darkness

The party of the Pharisees probably originated in persecution. Vicious, terrifying persecution marked the reign of Antiochus IV. The so-called Antiochus Epiphanes—he claimed to be a divine manifestation of the gods—ruled the Jews malevolently. Antiochus IV was determined to stamp out the Jewish religion. Any mother of a male baby who brought her newborn son to the temple for circumcision was liable to have both breasts amputated. This barbarity took place not infrequently.

It was dangerous to cling to the law of Moses in those days. To do so required a burning passion for Yahweh. But some men and women did have such a passion. More than this, the men devoted themselves to the study and teaching of that law and of their history and sacred books. Their courage was unquestionable, and their motives pure, for to do what they did required passion. They knew that the true and only God had revealed himself to them as a God of mercy, patience and longsuffering, and that he had promised them a Messiah. They knew he loved them personally. Therefore, taking the Word of God seriously, they ran the risk of their lives rather than deny him.

This is the way all movements of God's Holy Spirit start. God initiates them. Yet always they seem to go wrong later. Why do revivals peter out? Who knows?

The Pharisee movement in the first century A.D. had completely lost the spirit that had begun the movement more than two centuries earlier. The movement had changed radically, but the Pharisees of Jesus' day did not know it. Their minds had been darkened. Jesus, like John the Baptist who preceded him, saw the Pharisees as "a brood of vipers" (Mt 3:7). In Matthew 23:13-36 he curses them roundly, bitterly and repeatedly.[1] There was nothing of corporate holiness left in the movement. Passion was dead.

A few people such as Nicodemus, Joseph of Arimathea (who may or may not have been a Pharisee) and possibly Gamaliel were exceptions to the general rule. The movement itself, however, had become spiritually bankrupt, totally bereft of ardor. How did something whose origins were so good wind up opposed to God—and totally blind to the fact that it was so?

As we look at the two pictures of the Pharisees, the one in the rule of Antiochus Epiphanes and the other in Jesus' day, it becomes plain that by the time of Jesus they had gained enormously in prestige, popular influence and respect. And when people give you prestige and respect, it changes you. The end effect on the Pharisees was that they came to deserve Ezekiel's charges.

When I was a practicing psychiatrist some Christians viewed me with awe, believing that I could see right through them. I couldn't! Yet their adulation was like martinis to a drunk. Before long I began to think I must merit the respect I was getting. I lost sight of certain realities: first, their respect reflected the values of the society of that day, and second, I myself was no whit different from the way I had been when I wore a short white coat, the uniform of medical students. In any case I had lost sight of God, and of his goodness in allowing me to pass examinations and be in the privileged position of one who influences others. I thought I had a right to something *I* had earned. Darkness had descended on me. I was proud. I had forgotten that God was God. *And I had lost my passion for Jesus.*

Pride is deadly. It causes us to lose the sense of our eternal posture before God. To forget who God is, and therefore what our posture before him must always be, has tragic consequences. Paul explains it: "For although they knew God, they neither glorified him as God nor gave thanks to him, but their thinking became futile and their foolish hearts were darkened" (Rom 1:21).

People who have known God and yet have become proud are subject to psychological consequences. When they no longer glorify him as God or give thanks to him, darkness enshrouds them, and as it increases they lose their capacity to perceive reality. For that perception is based on our relationship with him. And the trouble with being in spiritual darkness is that you never know it, at least until the light dawns on you again. At that point you experience a sort of déjà vu and say, "Oh my stars! Whatever could have happened to me?" It is like waking from a nightmare. You may still be in need, but at least you know you are in need, whereas in the dark you did not know.

Be careful! Watch out! Paul addresses the Corinthian church like this: "Test yourselves to make sure you are solid in the faith. Don't drift along taking everything for granted. Give yourselves regular check-ups. You need firsthand evidence, not mere hearsay, that Jesus Christ is in you. Test it out. If you fail the test, do something about it" (2 Cor 13:5 TM).

The only valid test is the test of personal passion for Jesus.

The Conservative Evangelical Movement

I was born into the conservative evangelical movement, and still love it and feel a part of it. A review of its history is instructive. When liberal scholarship from Germany first became influential in Britain and Europe, the movement was divided between leaders who embraced the new scholarship and those who rejected it. Congregations were likewise divided.

The liberal side gained certain advantages. The better university posts were open to you if you could write papers or books drawing praise from "better" liberal scholars. Conservative scholars got lower posts, or no posts at all. Similarly, as a pastor or minister you had a better chance of getting a "good big" church if you could at least talk out of both sides of your mouth.

There was nothing that approximated the barbarity of the days of Antiochus Epiphanes. The whole affair was reasonably civilized and polite. But conservative evangelicals suffered. Like the early Pharisees they were willing to suffer for the Word of God and its principles. Thus a godly movement was born of men and women prepared to devote themselves to Scripture and even, if it should prove necessary, to penury. Some degree of ardor is necessary for such a stance.

Many conservative Christians accepted lower university posts, dedicating themselves to researching the very questions the liberals raised. Recognition began to come, and the scholarly value of their work was gradually acknowledged. Conservative publishing houses arose, and books were printed. The missionary impact of the movement was considerable. The movement had begun to earn respect, and its members could breathe again.

As the original leaders of the movement grew older, and many of them died, younger men, inspired by their example, began to take their place. But by this time the intellectual climate had changed considerably. There was prestige, if not wealth, attached to some seminary and even Bible school appointments. Spiritual darkness began to fall. Leaders became less like Jesus, who is the manifestation of the Father's holiness, and less in love with him. Evangelical scholarship had always been largely Calvinist; but as events in Azusa Street developed—with masses of low-income, less-educated people being influenced by the Pentecostal revival—the scholars' Calvinism became noticeably more Calvinist, clinging more tightly to its Reformed roots. All theology is reactionary to perceived error. And so God's movement among the poor was mostly disdained by evangelical leaders.

Here evangelicals had begun to break ranks with the Lord Jesus. For in his holiness Jesus *preferred* to be with the poor and needy, with his disciples and with his Father. Notice, it was his pleasure, his delight.

Though Jesus always carried out his duty, he was not duty-driven or conscience-haunted. He loved. He worked the works of God for the joy set before him. Because he loved, he enjoyed what he did. Curiously, and in spite of its pain, even the cross was a joy, for it was a gateway to glory. We refer to Jesus' death as his *passion*. His life and death were love-driven. Burning passion swept him by its driving power, hurtling him triumphantly into glory.

On earth Jesus knew there was a problem. The Pharisee leaders had imposed religious burdens on the backs of the Jewish people—burdens too great to bear. It is always thus. Oppression begins when holiness diminishes. In his introduction to Galatians, Eugene Peterson writes, "When men and women get their hands on religion, one of the first things they often do is turn it into an instrument for controlling others, either putting or keeping them 'in their place.' The history of such religious manipulation is long and tedious."[2]

Are conservative evangelical scholars passionately love-haunted, love-driven? Are they like Jesus? Or is the evolution of the movement well into the usual cycle? Would it be reasonable to expect the evangelical movement to be any different from movements that have preceded it? We too are human.

Passionate love is part of holiness. Doctrine alone cannot keep our hearts in the place God wants.

The Pentecostal Movement

As I read accounts of the early Pentecostal movement, no possible doubt remains in my mind that it was a movement born of God. Its story is one of glad abandonment to reckless passion. I do not mean that Pentecostals (any more than members of any other movement) were always free from doctrinal error. Errors abounded, but so they have done in all movements. Revivals of religion are messy things. Perhaps there was a mistaken notion about the importance of tongues. But what stands out, despite claims to the contrary, is that during the beginnings of the movement it could have been said, in the words of Matthew, "The blind receive sight, the lame walk, those who have leprosy are cured, the deaf hear, the dead are raised, and the good news is preached to the poor" (Mt 11:5).

The dead were raised? The blind received their sight? I believe so, though I recognize that there are two schools of thought regarding such things. Pentecostal literature of the time is either lying or truthful. I prefer to accept its truthfulness, because as I read it I detect the heartbeat of passion.

And with what effect the gospel was preached! The poor—the despised, the uneducated, society's rejects—turned to God in large numbers. A missionary movement of incomparable zeal was spawned. The faith and heroism of some of those early Pentecostal missionary efforts shames me profoundly.

But slowly the Pentecostals began to do exactly what the early Pharisees did, and what conservative evangelicals did. And I cannot criticize any movement for doing so. Pentecostals studied the Scriptures. They began to develop their own educational institutions. Later these same institutions sought accreditation, along with its financial advantages and spiritual dangers. Pentecostals know how to give, and do they ever give! Publishers came into existence, and books by Pentecostal authors became more polished. Withal came a growing respectability as well as growing acceptance in interdenominational "clubs" and associations. In retrospect it seems to have happened almost overnight.

One thing is certain. The Pentecostal movement in Europe and North America is no longer what it was. Like many a denomination it has forgotten its roots, and its founders would prove an embarrassment to the movement if they were to show up today. In this and other ways, it has all the marks of a middle-aged movement: prosperity, wealth and power. "You say, 'I am rich; I have acquired wealth and do not need a thing.' But you do not realize that you are wretched, pitiful, poor, blind and naked" (Rev 3:17).

Yes, by and large the Pentecostal movement has joined the club. For like the denominations that came to look with scorn upon their own beginnings, the hierarchy of Pentecostal groups today displays a certain hesitation about "the new boys on the charismatic block." Knowing seniors express grave doubts to one another about "the dangers of error"—or worse! Their expressions are reminiscent of things that leaders of other denominations used to say about the Pentecostal movement itself in its early days. Ah, respectability! Do we not all crave it? Holiness is rarely respectable for long. Passion never is. Human nature does not change. We are all fallen.

The sixties spawned a second movement, now dubbed the "second wave" of the Spirit, the Pentecostal movement being the first.[3] Though the charismatic movement shared the view of the baptism of the Spirit embraced by Pentecostals, it differed significantly in its beginnings, being more inclined, in North America anyway, to remain within established denominations and churches—Anglican, Episcopalian, Catholic and so on. It tended to reach more sophisticated groups. God had begun by showing mercy to the poor, to those nearest to his heart. But he had not forgotten the middle class, even some wealthy people. University students and graduate students were reached. God has mercy for everyone. We can all play a part.

Today the signs of evolutionary change among the "second-wavers" are more subtle and less measurable. But they are present. They are the marks of a movement that knows it is now established. There are publishing houses, literature, institutions and "ministries" always beginning well, then beginning to show the first signs of middle age. It is not merely that the old hands are themselves aging, for age brings needed experience. But the effects of self-congratulation are also present. And you cannot substitute earnestness for unspeakable and spontaneous joy in Christ.

Each wave—the first, the second and now the third—shows the same signs. Each began as a movement among youth. Each was certainly begun by God the Holy Spirit. Each has been affected by fallen human nature. Each is in danger of completing in the flesh what God began in the Spirit. Each brought the same message, that God wanted to restore to his people the gifts of the Spirit.

The Third Wave

In the third wave, of which I am grateful to be an (elderly) part, the trend shows itself in the tendency of prosperous pastors to pull out and do their own thing, and of some followers in the movement to feel superior to other groups. What else is new? We are dealing with fallen human nature, with sinful flesh. What God begins, human beings cannot finish. Yet to the third wave God has granted a singular grace.

By the time this book is published it will be fully recognized that events in the Toronto Airport Vineyard have had a worldwide impact. In this case, *the Holy Spirit is restoring passion.* God is awakening a burning passion in those who are genuinely touched. (Others may be so obsessed with themselves that all they can think of is that they have "got it"—whatever "it" may be. And usually in such cases they have become proud—like Satan himself.)

The manifestations that are featured so prominently are unimportant. John Wesley, I believe, made the mistake of giving too great importance to outward manifestations of the Spirit. He believed there were two calls of God on his life, the call to be a minister of the gospel and an "extraordinary call." To his brother Charles he once wrote, "My extraordinary call is witnessed by the work God doeth in my ministry; which proves he is with me of a truth in this exercise of my office."[4] Wesley was referring to how people often fell on the floor and cried out when the Holy Spirit came on them during his ministry. He felt this vindicated him in his call. Yet God was not vindicating Wesley, but his own name and reputation.

The same error persists today, as some leaders see similar manifestations as evidence of their superior spiritual power. The power was given by grace, not by merit. Yet God continues to be merciful to such leaders, even as they expose themselves to the danger of darkness. Human zeal can never accomplish the kind of things that are happening through the Toronto renewal. The devil tries to, but produces a poor counterfeit.

The Vineyard movement has nothing to be proud of. Once, asked how long it would be before the Vineyard movement ceased to be powerful and effective, John Wimber said, "Oh, about fifteen years!" If anything will save the Vineyard movement from following "the way of all flesh" it will be the grace of God, not the virtue of the movement's leaders and followers.

The prominence the press has given to the manifestations in Toronto and elsewhere is unfortunate, but understandable. The only thing that matters is the renewal of passionate love for God and for souls.

Corporate Holiness

But, you wonder, what does all this charismatic stuff have to do with holiness? Good question. *"Charismatic stuff" doesn't have anything to do with holiness. Or passion.* Rather, each time in history the Spirit is poured out afresh, whether God imparts spiritual gifts or not, a new devotion to Jesus is born—a new sense of his presence, a new awareness of his power and a new joy in evangelism. With every revival and renewal comes the rediscovery of a forgotten doctrine, whether of regeneration, repentance, justification by faith, trust in Christ or whatever.

God has spoken three times to the church in the twentieth century, with each of the three so-called waves of renewal. Three times he has told us that we need the gifts of the Holy Spirit to complete the evangelization of the world. The three waves have been outpourings of the Spirit of God. They are designed to equip the church for evangelization.

Let me make things clear. Having been present and examined personally the beginnings of both the second and the third waves, in North America and in various parts of the world, I can testify to three things. First, all three waves were of God. Second, all three, as in the past, have been outpourings of power to evangelize. Finally, all three have brought us the same message: God wants to restore the gifts of the Spirit to his people; and most of all, an ardent Lover wants ardor in return.

Outpourings such as the one that is spreading from Toronto are not outpourings of holiness. Yet as Lloyd-Jones pointed out, there are certainly "holy spinoffs." Joy and reawakened passion are two of them, "joy unspeakable and full of glory"—the joy of a passionate lover.

Not long ago Eleanor Mumford was preaching at Holy Trinity Church in Brompton, London. She told the story (which has been confirmed a number of times) of a woman who was driving home, still "drunk in the Spirit," after attending the Airport Vineyard. Her car was weaving on the freeway. Before long a police officer pulled her over. He said, "Ma'am, I believe you're very drunk."

She beamed and said. "You're darn right, I am! But not in the way you think!"

"I'm afraid I must give you a Breathalyzer test."

As the woman breathed into the officer's equipment, she burst into uncontrollable laughter and fell to the ground. For a moment the policeman stood frowning. Then, quite suddenly, he burst into helpless laughter himself. A moment or two later both of them could be observed rolling on the freeway, helplessly unable to control their laughter. Both were under the control of the Holy Spirit of God.

The officer said, "Lady, I don't know what it is you've got. But I sure need it." He was soundly converted shortly thereafter.

Bizarre? Yes. Though if we consider the way the woman "evangelized" the policeman, it certainly takes the "haunted conscience syndrome" out of personal evangelism.

Some of us are getting used to bizarre events. What matters—and this does have a bearing on corporate holiness—is that (and in this order) two things are being born: a passion for Jesus and also a passion for the lost. These passions are not born of pseudoearnestness, but of delirious joy! Joy of that magnitude is the wild enthusiasm of someone passionately in love.

For many people an experience of the Toronto sort is a start on the pathway of holiness. Unless that pathway is pursued—unless the passion is maintained, unless we spend time in heart-searching and confession of sin—the joy in evangelism will quickly fade, for holiness has to do with sharing the heart of Jesus. And the heart of Jesus is for the whole church.

13

UNITY & HISTORY'S END

*Aggiornamento [updating] does not only refer
to the renewal of the Church; nor only to the unification of
Christians, "that the world may believe" (Jn. 17:21).
It is also, and above all, God's saving activity
on behalf of the world.*
(*Pope John Paul II*, Crossing the Threshold of Hope)

*J*OHN 17 IS A PASSAGE OF UNUSUAL SIGNIFICANCE. WE CALL IT CHRIST'S HIGH priestly prayer in order to distinguish it from other chapters in the four Gospels. In this prayer Jesus declares that before he returns he will do something no organizing genius ever could do. He is going to create a degree of unity among his people that will render all church and denominational divisions irrelevant. He will create a heart unity among all his people.

This is no idealistic dream. Its fulfillment is sure. In the last part of John 17 Jesus calls on the Father to give him such a church as a bride.

In the closing verses of the chapter, beginning with verse 20, Jesus prays for the future church—*us*. Here he expresses the desires and ambitions he has for today's church. Out of the present ecclesiastical disunity he asks God to create perfect unity. Presumably he will carry this out with those who are willing to collaborate with him—that is, those who obey the Spirit's voice. He will do it. But he will do it with those who trust him.

My prayer is not for them alone. I pray also for those who will believe in me through their message, that all of them may be one, Father, just as you are in me and I am in you. May they also be in us so that the world may believe that you have sent me. (Jn 17:20-21)

The Ecclesiastical River

When I consider all the groups and organizations that name the name of Jesus Christ, I see a river. It is a long river and deep, which for two thousand years has been rolling through hills of surrounding nations. Nothing has ever stopped its flow, and new streams now flow into it. Storms threaten, but their rain will greatly add to its volume. However, I also see worldly pollution from its bed rising to its surface. In bubbles, streaks and oily smears, garbage and every manner of filth erupt throughout it. There for all the world to see is the foulness we wanted no one to know about. This river seems to bear no relation to Ezekiel's river.

Factories line the banks, emptying waste into the river—the world's empty and useless values. The river's waters are so poisoned with the pollution of sin and false worship that they cannot bring life. Dead fish float rotting on the surface. Gray grass and weeds eke out a sort of life at the river's edge. Trees beside it are gaunt and leafless skeletons. An enemy has been very, very busy. The ocean, though close, is still a distance away.

Stop to observe at a point somewhere in the second century. The river is already beginning to form a massive pseudodelta in a wide valley. Slowly it begins to break into innumerable branches of evil-smelling streams. Although these flow back together from time to time, the number of overall divisions increases as we follow the river downstream.

We the church have worshiped false gods, the gods of this age. Like Satan we are full of pride. Our hearts are hardened. God sighs and says, "Like the Jews into whom I grafted them, these people are a stiff-necked, hostile and rebellious bunch. I suppose there is nothing better than to let them reap what they are persistently sowing."

But a big change is coming. We are to be cleansed, made pure and united. "I have given them the glory that you gave me, that they may be one as we are one: I in them and you in me. May they be brought to complete unity to let the world know that you sent me and have loved them even as you have loved me" (Jn 17:22-23).

Christ gave us glory. Really? He gave it us that we might be one. Where has the glory gone? I see little evidence of it, though certainly it is evident in the Acts accounts of the early church. Will it return once we are united? God's purpose in giving it was that we might be united. Jesus' prayer is for complete unity, and the purpose of that unity is once again "to let the world know" the love of the Father for the Son. What scriptural reason could be of greater significance?

Trinitarian Unity Before Christ Returns

I declare that the kind of unity that exists in the Godhead will be formed in the church before the return of Christ, though whether it will precede Christ's return by a long or a short period I do not know. Unity will come because Jesus asked for it. It will happen before Christ returns because the purpose of unity is "that the world may believe you have sent me" (Jn 17:21). Will Christ's prayer be answered? Was there ever a prayer of Christ's that was *not* answered?

The world *must* see a united church. It is absolutely essential, in order that they may understand that Jesus Christ was truly sent by God the Father. I cannot overemphasize this fact.

Unity is little thought about today. Disenchanted by the utter failure of the World Council of Churches to achieve what it originally hoped to achieve, we are convinced (I hope) that only God can bring about real unity. We are to collaborate with *his* initiative, *his* timing, not try to do things because they are good. God alone knows the timing of his programs. The initiative must always be God's. Our role is that of colaborers. Unity cannot be and will not ever be wrought by Christian initiative alone.

For centuries we have seen approaches to such a unity in joint evangelistic efforts, but today the real goal seems further away than ever. Yet though any hope of unity at this stage seems wild, I believe it could happen in my own lifetime.

Unity means oneness of heart. Oneness is that which reconciles, and reconciliation is at the heart of the gospel's appeal. Oneness is likewise an expression of holiness. *We will not be one until a much greater measure of holiness pervades the church, and we shall never be even a relatively holy church until we are one body.*

Our divisions are largely based on differences of opinion about what the Bible teaches. Since truth is important, doctrinal differences are important. Curiously, the more the Scriptures are studied, the more divisions abound. This should tell us something. After all, we pride ourselves on building new study centers. However, most divisions have come about from the pride of the people involved in disputing whatever was being disputed. They were quarrels for control, quarrels based on self-righteousness. Satanic pride must be removed from us.

Many quarrels have resulted when leaders of the church abused their privilege to do exactly what Eugene Peterson talks about in his introduction to Galatians, which I quoted in chapter twelve: "When men and women get their hands on religion, one of the first things they often do is turn it into an instrument for controlling others, either putting or keeping them 'in their place.' "[1] Many leaders have turned truth into an instrument for controlling and subjugating men and women whom they should have been setting free. That is why clouds of judgment are gathering. We must welcome the clouds, though with dread and fear.

We have never come near the degree of oneness that Jesus' prayer conceives—"that all of them may be one, Father, *just as you are in me and I am in you*" (v. 21). I call this *trinitarian unity*. It is a unity of intimacy, of marriage passion. Quite obviously, human beings alone can never achieve it. But God can and will achieve it, along with those who are willing and humble enough to receive correction. The Father owes this to the Son, and will pay what he owes.

Jesus does not ask for an invisible unity. The world would never believe without seeing. He is asking for a day when the world will be forced to acknowledge that Jesus came from God and accomplished something that is humanly impossible—a united people. Human beings, I say, cannot organize such a thing. Have they not tried since the world began—or certainly since Babel was attempted? Neither force nor negotiation has ever achieved it. Endlessly we have pursued unity, but unity (with absolute freedom within it) is humanly impossible. Yet God promises such unity. And God can produce it. By his Spirit.

In what way are Father, Son and Spirit one? They are one in attitude, one in purpose, one in understanding and one in heart. Their hearts, as it were, beat as one. Their minds—totally unlike that of Siamese twins linked by a common brain—think as one. Yet they remain three and free—three distinct persons in one God, free in their love for one another. The Father loves and looks with pride on his unique Son. The Son, when he was on earth, made it his business to hear the Father's voice, watch what the Father was doing, be alert to the nuance in his every whisper. The Spirit, equally to be worshiped as God, carries out their wishes here and now, fulfilling their present plans on earth, watching over us with the Father's own tenderness, empowering and refreshing his church. He indwells us. Through and by him, both Father and Son indwell us, for he is also the Spirit of the Son and of the Father.

You don't understand it? Neither do I. But I muse on it daily and with wonder.

The Critical Spirit

What is at the core of all disunity? At its core lies something that I call a critical spirit. I will try to explain what I mean.

Unity must begin in the local church. You cannot have a united church if you do not have united congregations. In fact, unity begins wherever the individual is. It begins in the smallest units in the church. Unity in the church begins with unity in one family. Wherever I am, wherever you are, that is the starting place for unity.

What is it, then, that creates disunity in you or in me? Unity begins to be corroded whenever we think critical thoughts of someone. In Mike Mason's superb study of the book of Job, he points out what should be obvious to us, the strange legalistic understanding of God that Job's three friends have. Job and the three friends seem to be monotheists—to worship one God. (Polytheism and monism both are pagan derivatives of theism. Therefore we need not be surprised that Job and his friends are theists.) But among them only Job understands the pardoning grace of God, even though Messiah would not come for centuries:

I know that my Redeemer lives,
    and that in the end he will stand upon the earth.
And after my skin has been destroyed,
    yet in my flesh I will see God;
I myself will see him

with my own eyes—I, and not another.
How my heart yearns within me! (Job 19:25-27)
The critical, gossiping spirit reigning in most churches effectively destroys the understanding that Job had. Criticism of others is deadly. Consider Jesus' words to his disciples—and let me translate his verb *krino* as "criticize" instead of the more usual translation, "judge." (For discussion of this translation issue, see the appendix.)

Do not criticize, and you will not be criticized. Do not condemn, and you will not be condemned. Forgive, and you will be forgiven. (Lk 6:37)

The words are true in an eschatological sense. In a coming day God will employ precisely such criteria in dealing with our criticisms. But they are also true existentially, in a psychological sense. Critical people begin to live in an unreal world peopled by their critical enemies. They become paranoid: "Did you see the way she looked at me? I wonder why she looked at me like that." "You know, I don't like the way he said that. There was a meaning behind his words." We become the victims of our own critical attitude.

"The teachers of the law and the Pharisees sit in Moses' seat," Jesus said (Mt 23:2). We too "sit in Moses' seat" when we criticize other people and other churches. We assume prerogatives that do not belong to us. We mimic those whom Jesus cursed.

Job's friends adopted the same stance. Picture them sitting beside him for a week, appalled at the severity of his sufferings. But even as they sit they are puzzled. *There must be something profoundly wrong with him,* they think. *God would never do this for nothing.*

It is a distasteful fact, but a fact nonetheless, that the same three friends who came "to sympathize with [Job] and to comfort him" 2:11, were in their minds picking him to pieces, analyzing him up and down for faults, loopholes and hidden sins, casting around in search of reasons for all the terrible things that had happened to him. And although we are told that these discreet gentlemen said nothing at all to Job for an entire week, is it not probable that they whispered confidentially among themselves?[2]

Yet it is not for his sins that Job suffers, but for his righteousness (Job 1:8; 2:3). To be sure, he does not fully understand the God he adores, and later he is forced to admit this (42:1-6). Yet the fact remains that it is for his integrity and his righteousness that he suffers. His friends fail utterly to grasp this.

Feeling overwhelmed, and scrambling to get a better fix on the problem, they will do the only safe thing: they will pull back and assume the stance of objective analysts. Naturally they will go about all of this in a very warm and godly way and with the best of intentions. . . . Yet without realizing it, by their clinical theorizing they are effectively withdrawing their human affections, and this at the very time when this is most needed. . . . Like all fair-weather friends, and all flawed theology, Job's friends stop short of the cross.[3]

Costing Everything, yet Free

The way of the cross is a very painful way. It costs us everything we have. But is "everything we have" really so valuable?

Bitterness weighs nothing but corrodes our guts like acid. Soon there will be nothing left of us but the stench. Let's get rid of "everything we have," bitterness included.

"What—after what she said to me?"

Yes, yes, yes! Get rid of it! Above all, get rid of a spirit that condemns others. To cling is to shrivel, to grow smaller and smaller. You could become a one-dimensional full stop, bleating your new form of worship, "Me, me, me!" when all the time God is waiting to give you glory.

But if we never criticize, how will things be put right? If we close our eyes and "see no evil" or cover our ears to avoid hearing it, how will matters mend? Let me get back to the verse on judging—or *criticizing*. Remember how God views you. He offered you free pardon. There were no strings attached—except that you receive what was offered. If you didn't receive what was offered, you don't have it. But if you did receive it, then you owe it to others.

Yes, but don't some people have to be disciplined out of the church? If they will not receive forgiveness, yes. But what is at the heart of church discipline? Not to receive forgiveness is not only the only crime, but the greatest. We discipline the brother or sister *who will not accept help*.

Still, how can we offer forgiveness without being critical?

The True Nature of Discernment

Jesus taught us that we cannot see clearly when we criticize. We have "a plank in our eye."

Why do you look at the speck of sawdust in your brother's eye and pay no attention to the plank in your own eye? . . . You hypocrite, first take the plank out of your own eye, and then you will see clearly to remove the speck from your brother's eye. (Mt 7:3, 5)

Then you will see clearly . . . A critical attitude destroys clarity of vision. Of course we must see. But we are to see with the eyes of Christ. Our own vision is distorted. We have planks that falsify our view of others. First we must drop our critical feelings and be filled with forgiveness—Christ's forgiveness toward us, and ours toward the rest of humankind; then we will see clearly.

Can we forgive before "they" repent? What matters is our attitude. As we see others we are to be *armed with love and forgiveness.* That is how God views us. He did not wait for repentance before sending his Son to die. It was our very lack of repentance that killed the Son—the Sacrifice!

Only when we are armed with God's attitude will God give us words of liberation for others, setting them so free that they will not become defensive or guarded. They will embrace us and weep with joy and gladness.

Repeatedly I find that when I approach my fellow church members with only love in my heart (it happens rarely, but repeatedly), they begin to share their problems with me. At some point then I seem to have what some would call a flash of illumination, and others the voice of the Spirit. In that moment I say, "I think you behave as you do because . . ." Suddenly we are in each other's arms, and my friend is weeping—weeping at the wonder of the discovery. He does not see my words as criticism, but as a means of being set free.

Let us then behold the glory of Christ. In beholding it we will begin to share it. And in beholding it we will cease to criticize our brothers and sisters. Eugene Peterson gets it right in the way he translates Ephesians 5. We need to share the quality of the love of God revealed in Christ:

Watch what God does, then do it, like children learn proper behavior from their parents. Mostly what God does is love you. Keep company with him and learn a life of love. Observe how Christ loved us. His love was not cautious, but extravagant. He didn't love in order to get something from us but to give everything of himself to us. Love like that. (vv. 1-2 TM)

God's love toward us sets us free. It sets us free to love. When we love we see clearly, but without critical feelings. We "judge with righteous judgment."

Our Hope for the Future

Unity is coming whether we decide to go for it or not. If we should choose to go for it, we will be collaborating with Christ.

But this unity is eschatological, in that it is going to take place either at the end or at "the beginning of the end." I suspect that "the beginning of the end" is fairly close—but nothing has fooled people more, or more frequently, than end-time predictions. Still, it has to happen sometime! Sooner or later God will have his way, and we shall be one. He will have his way with or without your collaboration and mine—but with the collaboration of some.

Certainly a far greater degree of unity will follow Israel's repentance, their mourning over their Messiah. At the point at which I am writing, this has not yet taken place on any major scale. What *is* happening is a worldwide outpouring of God the Holy Spirit in various forms, and at a point that is unique in human history. A far greater degree of unity has to come about before Christ's personal return, as I said earlier, since the purpose of unity is to convince the world of Jesus' identity. When the church (and Israel) are one, the world will believe. And until the church is one the world will not believe. We cannot take the initiative in the matter, but I have a feeling that God is now doing so.

The Uniqueness of This Historical Period

Is our period in history in any sense unique? If so, what is new in the world situation?

We can now destroy most of the world's population in a few seconds. This was never before possible. In addition, never before have we been able to hear what is going on elsewhere in the world, sometimes in minutes. Communication links bewilder and almost strangle us. Never before have such things been. We can travel to most places on the globe in less than twenty-four hours—often in luxury. The rate of knowledge-accumulation has never been so rapid. New discoveries have been made throughout history, but never before have people's lives and fates been so linked to everybody else's by computer. Never has knowledge been so great, nor solutions to world problems so complex.

Given these realities, our hopes should surely rise, if we believe the Puritans. For the Puritans taught that these sorts of things would precede Christ's return.

In part 1 of his *History of Redemption* Jonathan Edwards, having commented on the verse "Then began men to call upon the name of the Lord" as a sign of the activity of God's Spirit, continues, "It may here be observed, that from the fall of man to our day, the work of redemption in its effect has mainly been carried on by remarkable communications of the Spirit of God. . . . The way in which the greatest things have been done . . . [has] been by remarkable effusions, at special seasons of mercy."[4]

Edwards had embarked on the task of writing a history of the church. But like the Reformers, he sees the history of redemption as one history, and the church as beginning at the dawn of history. He opens the introduction to his book with these words: "The design of this chapter is to comfort the church under her sufferings, and the persecution of her enemies; and the argument of consolation . . . is the constancy and perpetuity of God's mercy . . . protecting her against all assaults of her adversaries."[5]

All over the world the church needs comfort. As we face the appalling rise of crime and see nations teetering on the brink of another world war, we could do with real comfort. And in many parts of the world persecution of God's people is open and vicious. Even in the West fashions are rapidly changing, and Christians—sometimes deservedly, sometimes not—are slowly seeing their liberties eroded. The church in the "Christian" West is no longer popular.

Martyrdom is part of the church's traditional lot. But there is salvation in the midst of death, the saving presence of our God even when we face death by martyrdom. Our hope has nothing to do with physical death, except that we are assured of victory in death.

Martyrdom will be a small price to pay for the future we expect. Earlier I summarized current world situations that are unique. But I failed to mention the most wonderfully unique situation of all. Never before in world history, nor in the history of the church, have revivals been starting in every part of the world at once. And all the Reformers anticipated such a time.

Either we are approaching our doom, or else we are on the eve of something far more wonderful. The key to what will happen is to be found in God's dealings with his own people—Israel and the church. Unity among God's people will presage widespread blessing and gospel triumph throughout the earth.

Again I ask: Did [the Jews] stumble so as to fall beyond recovery? Not at all! Rather, because of their transgression, salvation has come to the Gentiles to make Israel envious. But if their transgression means riches for the world, and their loss means riches for the Gentiles, how much greater riches will their fullness bring! (Rom 11:11-12)

Because the world situation is unique, because revival seems to be in its initial stages worldwide, and because the political pressures on the nation of Israel are reaching a new high, I believe that the beginning of the end is upon us. Can this really be what is happening? Could this be *it*—the beginning of what the Puritans were expecting and predicting from Scripture? Consider some of the passages quoted by Iain Murray in his book *The Puritan Hope*. They thrill my heart.

William Jay, 1769-1853. We have many and express assurances in the Scriptures, which cannot be broken, of the . . . universal spread and reign of Christianity, which are not yet accomplished. Nothing has yet taken place in the history of Divine grace, wide enough in extent, durable enough in continuance, powerful enough in energy, blessed enough in enjoyment, magnificent enough in glory, to do anything like justice to these predictions and promises.

John Owen, 1616-1683. Though our *persons* fall, our *cause* shall be as truly, certainly, and infallibly be victorious, as that Christ sits at the right hand of God. The gospel shall be victorious. This greatly comforts and refreshes me.

Thomas Goodwin, 1600-1679. There will come a time when the generality of mankind, both Jew and Gentile, shall come to Jesus Christ. He hath had but little takings of the world yet, but he will have before he hath done.[6]

The Puritans, very understandably, did not generally include in this "Jew and Gentile" vision the notion that Eastern and Western (Roman) churches would be united in one glorious body. To them, and again very understandably, the Roman Catholic Church appeared as Babylon and the Great Whore. But in the same way that God preserved for himself a hundred prophets in the northern kingdom of Israel (1 Kings 18:4), so also he has preserved essential doctrines *through* the Roman Catholic and Eastern churches and has always had true believers *within* both. Their numbers (in the Roman Catholic Church especially) now are greater than they have ever been.

As signs of early revival multiply throughout the earth, then, my hopes awaken in a way they have never done before. The gospel, I believe, is about to prevail throughout the earth. The church is about to become one in a way it never before has.

But first will come division—in every church and denomination. For there are those who know everything already and need no further instruction. And there are others in every church and denomination who have awakened to the awareness that they do not know everything and that they are in need (1 Jn 2:27). It is between these broad groups that division, preceding final unity, will come. Some will reject the outpouring of God's Spirit. Others will reach out for it.

And I say, let's get it all over with! Let the final divisions and the terrible judgments come! I am under no illusions as to their appalling nature, but since they have to come, let us get them over with. Glory is to follow—great glory, the glory of Christ and the triumph of the gospel he died for. The gospel will triumph to a degree that it never has before. That triumph will be "wide enough in extent, durable enough in continuance, powerful enough in energy, blessed enough in enjoyment, magnificent enough in glory" (to repeat William Jay's words) to fulfill every prophecy you could wish for. Peace on earth will be true peace. And whether Christ shall reign in bodily presence (as some believe) or for now through his people, I for one am willing to have it either way.

So with all my heart I cry, "Even so come, Lord Jesus!"

Appendix

DISCERNING TRUTH FROM FALSITY

*S*ome people say, "The Holy Spirit would never cause division." This assumption is false. We are in the midst of a divisive controversy now—and this is only one of many such controversies throughout church history. Debate arises especially whenever the Spirit of God is poured out. Why is that?

Jesus himself told us while he was here on earth. He said,

Do not suppose that I have come to bring peace to the earth. I did not come to bring peace, but a sword. For I have come to turn

a man against his father,

a daughter against her mother,

a daughter-in-law against her mother-in-law—

a man's enemies will be the members of his own household. (Mt 10:34-36)

The greatest outpouring of God's Spirit to date occurred when God the Son came to earth as the Son of Man. Terrible religious division tore God's people apart. The wound has yet to be healed. That division and its aftermath resulted in the death, resurrection and ascension of Christ, and the persecution of the church for two millennia.

And divisions arise even among Christians. When violent disputes occur among God's people, we discern truth by following those Scriptures that teach discernment. Discernment of truth and falsity is dealt with repeatedly in the New Testament. Preachers and teachers are seen as prophets (false or true) in several passages (such as 1 Jn 4:1). All preaching should be prophetic in the sense of bringing God's people a message from God—a message for the hour, or the day, in which the preacher preaches. Prophetic preaching in the midst of controversy, then, is preaching that purports to address the serious questions of the day. We need discernment to distinguish false preaching from true preaching.

Judgment and Criticism

Key to the understanding of how we distinguish the false from the true is the use of the verb *krinō* (judge) in Scripture. From *krinō* come our English words *criticize* and *criticism*. In the New Testament the word is generally translated "judge." A judge uses his *critical* faculties to interpret the law in relation to the person being judged. He assesses two things, the prisoner and ideas about the prisoner—the ideas expounded and expressed in the form of law. Thus he assesses both people and ideas about people, both the prisoner and how the law applies to the prisoner.

Scripture makes it plain that when we see wrongs in the church or the world, we must distinguish between people and ideas. We are to criticize ideas, but we are to love people. We criticize murder but love the murderer. We must condemn thieving but love the thief, condemn adultery but love the adulterer. Most of us do the very opposite. We are sloppy in our thinking about ideas, but we feel we are discerning about people. We are not. We confuse criticism with discernment. We criticize people, and we fail to think carefully.

Remember *krinō* can mean both "judge" and "criticize." We must first beware of having a critical spirit. Such a spirit destroys discernment. Our criticism comes to be directed at persons, rather than at the false teaching that certain teachers may exemplify. Jesus himself explains how this destroys discernment:

Why do you look at the speck of sawdust in your brother's eye and pay no attention to the plank in your own eye? How can you say to your brother, "Brother, let me take the speck out of your eye," when you yourself fail to see the plank in your own eye? You hypocrite, first take the plank out of your eye, and then you will see clearly to remove the speck from your brother's eye. (Lk 6:41-42)

Jesus also makes it clear that he alone has the right to pronounce judgment. All judgment has been committed to him. He tells us that "the Father judges no one, but has entrusted all judgment to the Son" (Jn 5:22). Therefore when we presume to assess and condemn others *we are taking over the task of deity.*

There is only one context in which we may judge others. It is in the context of governing the local church. When quarrels arise in a local congregation, the dispute should be settled "in house." And even then we must be very careful not to have a condemning spirit. We are to love would-be litigants.

In 1 Corinthians 6 Paul pours scorn on the idea that we should submit to the judgment of a human law court. Most people who do so are out for their rights, sometimes even vengeance. But if one day we are to judge angels . . .

If any of you has a dispute with another, dare he take it before the ungodly for judgment instead of before the saints? Do you not know that the saints will judge the world? And if you are to judge the world, are you not competent to judge trivial cases? (1 Cor 6:1-2)

What Jesus calls us to give up is a *critical attitude.* A critical attitude is inconsistent both with love and, as we have seen, with true discernment. Because the verb *krinō* can equally well be translated "criticize" or "condemn," we could express Matthew 7:1-2 as follows: "Do not criticize, or you too will be criticized. For in the same way you criticize others, you will be criticized, and with the measure you use, it will be measured to you."

In what sense will we be criticized if we indulge in criticism? In two senses. First, in a coming day, at Christ's judgment seat, we will find our behavior held up for a critical review. But second, in the present we will discover that the habit of criticizing others reaps a more immediate "reward." We begin to adjust our behavior to avoid criticism. We also become more suspicious of the reactions of people around us. We read into innocent words and gestures meanings that are not implied. In a word, a critical attitude tends to make us paranoid. A "paranoid personality" is usually a very critical person.

Danger! Beware!

Notice that the Bible warns *repeatedly* about Satan's activity in opposing all outpourings of his Spirit. It warns particularly against false teachers, sometimes referred to as false prophets. Consider the words of Christ: "Watch out for false prophets. They come to you in sheep's clothing, but inwardly they are ferocious wolves" (Mt 7:15-16).

Beware! Watch out! We use such words in an emergency, sometimes shouting them as a warning. Christ may have spoken his warning quietly, but there is a deadly seriousness to his words. The concern he raises is of the utmost gravity. We all are called on to make a decision. Our eternal destiny may be at stake. But what exactly is the danger?

The danger lies in one of the two sides involved in a controversy. The true side is safe, the false side dangerous. So to choose the right side is critical for each one of us. False prophets are described as wolves in sheep's clothing. They appear to be very safe. We find ourselves having great confidence in their words. They soothe us, bring us reassurance and relief. Yet precisely there lies the danger.

"Inwardly they are ferocious wolves!" The demeanor of such leaders is meant to entrap us in a false security. It is a deception of Satan that could place our feet on a perilous pathway. Ravening wolves devour sheep. Sheep are foolish creatures, easily deceived. Jesus, as the Good Shepherd, is sounding the alarm. He alone is the doorway for the sheep. His words are the only ones that bring safety in a time of great danger.

By their fruit you will recognize them. Do people pick grapes from thornbushes, or figs from thistles? Likewise every good tree bears good fruit, but a bad tree bears bad fruit. A good tree cannot bear bad fruit, and a bad tree cannot bear good fruit. Every tree that does not bear good fruit is cut down and thrown into the fire. Thus, by their fruit you will recognize them. (Mt 7:17-20)

"You will know false prophets—like trees—by their fruits," Jesus tells us plainly. The false prophet gives a false message. The true prophet gives a true message. The false prophet leads the sheep into danger. The true prophet brings them to food and shelter, rest and safety. The vital question then concerns the fruit of each prophet's ministry.

Take the example of the controversy raging (as I write) over what one side calls manifestations of the Holy Spirit and what some people on the other side call manifestations of an unholy spirit. It is important to be sure we are following truth. How do we tell which side is correct? Certainly not by the manifestations themselves, which could mean absolutely anything. We tell by the fruits of the message. To repeat the words of Eleanor Mumford in London, "It's not how you go down [fall on the floor] that matters, but how you come up."

Remember also Steve, the pastor who spoke to me in slurred speech after a day or two of "drunkenness in the Spirit." He tried to explain on the telephone, but soon I was listening to a long silence. His wife had to say, "Sorry, John! Perhaps if you call tomorrow . . ." Steve was unconscious on the floor.

What Steve eventually said was "John, I've never worshiped the Lord like this before. Ever since this started, the sense of the Lord's presence has been so real! I fall asleep worshiping him, and my first thought on waking is to praise him and love him." Steve's love for the Scriptures and for prayer had greatly increased. His urgency to reach out to the lost had been multiplied, whether "the lost" were wandering, bewildered Christians or unsaved men, women and children. He had also been empowered, so that subsequent evangelistic efforts in Canada, Russia and Brazil were successful, whereas before they had been difficult and labored. And Steve is only one of an ever-increasing number of people who have been so affected.

Perhaps the very virulence of the attack on this kind of "drunken" experience reflects Satan's fear that his time is now very short. *"You will know them by their fruits."* You don't gather grapes from thornbushes. Thornbushes scratch and tear you if you get tangled up in them. You recognize a thornbush (or a wolf) by what it produces. Similarly we are to judge what is truly the work of the Holy Spirit by both its immediate and its long-term fruits.

False prophets are the real fomenters of division and criticism in the body of Christ. They make personal attacks. The Sadducees and the Pharisees were not able to rest until they had Jesus on the cross. Even there they reviled him. And when in their hearts they knew from the soldiers' testimony that he had risen from the dead, they bribed those same soldiers to give a false account of what had happened.

All of us should teach carefully. We must evaluate ideas, not people. True prophets do not make personal attacks. We should name the teaching and evaluate it for good points and bad, contrasting true ideas with false, true doctrines with error. To mention people, to pronounce their names, serves no good purpose. What we should rather do is teach our congregations how to assess ideas. We are to equip saints, not destroy them.

False prophets will always be shown to be false in the end. The common source of scandal surrounding false prophets is the abuse of money, of sex and of the power they have wielded. Their end is seldom delayed long.

But for many followers, the exposure of false teaching will come too late. We must decide *now*. Neutrality carries the same dangers as being wrong.

The world scene is confusing. News programs do not always focus on the core realities that underlie events. For me, the core reality is the answer to the question "What is the sovereign God doing at the moment?" For he is in charge, isn't he?

Is what some people call renewal God's judgment on the church or his blessing? Admittedly, as John Wimber points out, not everything that accompanies a renewal movement is the activity of the Holy Spirit. Some of it is the response of disturbed humanity. Manifestations of the Holy Spirit and pseudomanifestations may be mixed, presenting a very confusing picture. *But we know by fruit.* What matters is the health of the church a year later, and ten years later.

The Serious Nature of the Question

Anyone who speaks a word against the Son of Man will be forgiven, but anyone who speaks against the Holy Spirit will not be forgiven, either in this age or in the age to come. (Mt 12:32)

These are words of Jesus—and they are terrifying words. Apparently there is one sin that will never be forgiven—never, never, never. For centuries commentators have groped for an explanation of this verse. Those that I have read seem not to grasp the significance of the occasion on which the words were uttered. Jesus had just cast out a demon. *Kingdom power had been manifest*—there had just been a release of supernatural kingdom power over against the devil's limited power. The Holy Spirit's power had been shown to be superior to the devil's.

The Pharisees had attributed the release to an unholy spirit. In effect, they had called God the devil. To do so is a grievous affront.

The verse awakens very great fear in me. I must curb all criticism within myself, lest I fall into this shocking error. I hope Jesus means that the "unpardonable sin" is *persistently* and repeatedly calling God the devil. But even this I do not know. The reality of the danger sends chills up my spine.

Are the people Christ speaks of not Christians to start with? Are they possibly tares rather than wheat? Who knows? In any case, *we are not to judge, criticize or condemn others.* We are to think in terms of ideas—of the terrible danger of doing something that cannot and will never be forgiven.

Distorting the Truth

The apostle Peter tackles the same issue of how we are to discern in his second epistle. In the first two verses of chapter 2 he tells us that in just the same way as false prophets once arose, false teachers will arise—and have now arisen. His words, like those of Christ, startle and chill us as he goes on:

> In their greed these teachers will exploit you with stories they have made up. Their condemnation has long been hanging over them, and their destruction has not been sleeping. . . . But these men blaspheme in matters they do not understand. They are like brute beasts, creatures of instinct, born only to be caught and destroyed, and like beasts they too will perish. (2 Pet 2:3, 12)

The blasphemy of these false teachers seems to be speaking against celestial beings. It is a solemn thing to call God the devil. What are the "stories they have made up"? Distortions of truth, manifesting the Satanic ability to select only portions of the truth, framing them in a way calculated to deceive. It is the art of out-of-context quotes and incidents.

Peter's warning does not awaken a desire to point fingers in condemnation, but to cry out to God for mercy on any preachers who are in danger of doing this. Hell is no figment of imagination but a terrible reality of outer darkness, inward pain and frustration—an eternal regret that can never be resolved.

One lust common among false preachers and teachers, as Peter points out, is greed. Greed will always be deceptive. Money makes us feel safe. To feel safe is to feel we are on the right side. But in the end we will be forced to see what we have seen in the past: that money, sex and power are the principal sources of a preacher's (or a prophet's) downfall.

Learning Discernment

As I read the Scriptures I am convinced that our business is not to criticize others or to point fingers, but *to teach the body of Christ how to distinguish false and true for themselves.* We must not merely assert, frantically, our own correctness. This is exactly what false teachers and prophets do. Instead we must teach principles. We must impart discernment. This is what Jesus, Peter and John are doing.

John seems to devote most of the fourth chapter of his first epistle to this task. Like Jesus, he refers to the false teachers as false (or pseudo) prophets: "Dear friends, do not believe every spirit, but test the spirits to see whether they are from God, because many false prophets have gone out into the world" (1 Jn 4:1).

When John tells us to "test the spirits" he is not exactly telling us how to detect demons. Rather, he is referring to the spirits inspiring false prophets. In a particular case the spirit may well be a powerful demon. Or it could be the prophet's own spirit.

Obviously we are not required to go up to a false prophet with the intention of casting out any such demon—even if we are convinced the demon exists. To do so would be inappropriate for many reasons.

But we are to be discerning. We are to test the spirits, and immediately John gives us the preliminary, or the most basic, test of all—a test many false prophets seem to pass easily: does the prophet teach that Jesus came in the flesh? "This is how you can recognize the Spirit of God: Every spirit that acknowledges that Jesus Christ has come in the flesh is from God, but every spirit that does not acknowledge Jesus is not from God" (1 Jn 4:2-3).

Charles Chauncey, who bitterly opposed both Jonathan Edwards and George Whitefield in the Great Awakening, proclaimed Christ's divinity—at first. His books sold widely, whereas Edwards's writings, now so revered by scholars, were largely ignored. But Chauncey had entered into darkness by opposing Edwards and Whitefield. He wound up as a Unitarian—one who denies that Jesus Christ came in the flesh as the God-man. God's Word stands true.[1]

Today's critics do exactly what Chauncey did, and could end up as he did. Certainly their behavior suggests *deistic* rather than *theistic* beliefs,[2] and holding deistic assumptions is the first step toward denying the physical nature of divine Messiah's coming.

The test John describes is only the very beginning. It is possible to profess a conventional belief but to have a heart far from God. John has already warned about this in chapter 2 of his first epistle: "If someone claims, 'I know him well!' but doesn't keep his commandments, he's obviously a liar. His life doesn't match his words. . . . Anyone who claims to live in God's light and hates a brother or sister is still in the dark" (1 Jn 2:4, 9 TM).

In chapter 4 John continues by focusing attention, not now on the false prophets, but on the true. What are the fruits in the life of a true prophet? Already from Steve's testimony and from the words of Eleanor Mumford we have an idea of them. John the apostle continues, but first he gives us a word of assurance: "We are from God, and whoever knows God listens to us; but whoever is not from God does not listen to us. This is how we recognize the Spirit of truth and the spirit of falsehood" (1 Jn 4:6).

The division, he tells us, is between truth and falsehood. Those whom God has already chosen will listen to our word. *As we see the light on their faces, we will receive an assurance that yes, we are on the right track*. But is this all John has to tell us? No. There is much he adds, for there is a test by which we may secretly determine whether those who profess to believe that Jesus is God's Son really do believe. For belief is a matter of the heart (the whole person), not just the head.

If anyone acknowledges that Jesus is the Son of God, God lives in him and he in God. And so we know and rely on the love God has for us.

God is love. Whoever lives in love lives in God, and God in him. . . . We love because he first loved us. (1 Jn 4:15-16, 19)

Only a true acknowledgment of Jesus results in love. As we saw in 1 John 2:9, this means love and not hate for brothers and sisters. Only such an acknowledgment springs from the Father. Heart belief will at length bring deepening assurance that we are loved by God. Genuine awareness of that love, in turn, will cause us to love others. Thus true faith in Christ (as distinct from intellectual assent to a theological proposition) will eventually issue in a love of all humankind. "If anyone says, 'I love God,' yet hates his brother, he is a liar. For anyone who does not love his brother, whom he has seen, cannot love God, whom he has not seen. And he has given us this command: Whoever loves God must also love his brother" (1 Jn 4:20-21).

As I listened to a tape of Eleanor Mumford's testimony in London, I realized the truth of these words of John. Eleanor was so much in love with Jesus and with those around her that she was, she said, "just mad to lay my hands on people!"

The love God wants to give us is a passionate, mad, crazy love, a love that will drive us to the ends of the earth for Jesus. We will not care about ourselves, *our* reputation, *our* wealth, *our* power. All we will want is to be like him and do what he did. We will simply long, like Paul, to know Christ the only way he can be known—"to know Christ and the power of *his* resurrection and the fellowship of sharing in *his* sufferings, becoming *like him* in his death" (Phil 3:10).

Notes

Part One: The Descent into Holiness
[1]John White, *Changing on the Inside* (Ann Arbor, Mich.: Servant, 1991).
[2]Laughter, weeping, falling on the floor, roaring like lions, shaking and other such manifestations are commonplace.

Chapter 1: The Need for Holiness
[1]My emphasis. J. I. Packer, "God," in *New Dictionary of Theology*, ed. S. F. Ferguson, D. F. Wright and J. I. Packer (Leicester, U.K.: Inter-Varsity Press, 1988), p. 277.
[2]C. S. Lewis, *The Voyage of the Dawn Treader* (New York: Macmillan, 1970).
[3]William R. Moody, *The Life of D. L. Moody by His Son* (New York: Fleming H. Revell, 1900), p. 149.
[4]Anne R. Cousin, "O Christ, What Burdens."
[5]J. I. Packer, *Knowing God*, rev. ed. (Downers Grove, Ill.: InterVarsity Press, 1993), pp. 179-99. The full story is found in Homer's *Iliad*.
[6]John R. W. Stott, *The Cross of Christ* (Downers Grove, Ill.: InterVarsity Press, 1986), p. 169.
[7]Packer, *Knowing God*, p. 189.
[8]Subsequently, though terribly angry over what God had done, David seems to have realized that a cart was hardly the appropriate form of transportation for God. Carrying the ark on the shoulders of the Levites, as God had commanded Moses, symbolized the direction of Israel by the Holy Spirit of God.
[9]John Bunyan, *The Pilgrim's Progress* (London: Lutterworth, 1947), p. 20.
[10]I have adapted several sections of this chapter, from the heading "The Gospel of Propitiation" to this point, from my article "Good News About an Angry

God" in the Vineyard magazine, *Equipping the Saints,* Second Quarter 1995, pp. 16-17.

Chapter 2: Scripture Truth as a Guide to Holiness
[1]Jack Deere, *Surprised by the Power of the Spirit* (Grand Rapids, Mich.: Zondervan, 1993), p. 47.

[2]John Piper, *The Pleasures of God* (Portland, Ore.: Multnomah Press, 1991), p. 123.

[3]The Bible seems clear enough about the sinfulness of homosexuality. It is "an abomination" (Lev 18:22; 20:13). Each time the statement is made in a context clear of any reference to male and female temple prostitution. In Romans 1 Paul refers to homosexuality as part of God's judgment on humankind, his "giving over" of men and women to certain behaviors because they did not honor God as God. Thus Paul implies that our bodies were not designed for such a use. A very full discussion of homosexuality can be found in John White, *Eros Redeemed* (Downers Grove, Ill.: Intervarsity Press, 1993), chaps. 10-11.

[4]Cedric B. Johnson, *The Psychology of Biblical Interpretation* (Grand Rapids, Mich.: Zondervan, 1983), pp. 41-42.

[5]You may say, "Hey! Hold on a minute! You can't start telling people to change their church!" No, and I do not even try to. All church-hopping is out. My own policy is to stick with my church until they throw me out for heresy. Until that time I stay.

[6]A quotation from Dan Hamilton, *The Beggar King* (Downers Grove, Ill.: InterVarsity Press, 1993), p. 107.

[7]J. I. Packer, *Knowing God,* rev. ed. (Downers Grove, Ill.: InterVarsity Press, 1993), p. 36.

[8]Richard Baxter, *The Saints' Everlasting Rest* (Grand Rapids, Mich.: Baker Book House, 1978), p. 359.

[9]Packer, *Knowing God,* p. 36.

[10]John Bunyan, *Grace Abounding* (Chicago: Moody Press, 1959), pp. 45-46.

[11]Ibid.

Chapter 3: Deliverance from the Darkness of Pride
[1]Philip Dodderidge (1702-1751), *The Rise and Progress of Religion in the Soul* (Grand Rapids, Mich.: Baker Book House), p. 46.

[2]A. W. Tozer, *The Pursuit of God* (Camp Hill, Penn.: Christian Publications, 1982), pp. 109-10.

[3]C. S. Lewis, *Mere Christianity* (New York: Collier Books, 1952), p. 109.

[4]Ibid., pp. 109-10.

[5]Ibid., p. 111.

[6]Ibid., p. 114.

[7]Don Williams, "Living with the Free Jesus," *Equipping the Saints,* Fourth Quarter 1994, p. 7 (quoted from *Jesus and Addiction* [Recovery Books]).

Chapter 4: The Necessity of Repentance

[1]Fanny J. Crosby, "Rescue the Perishing."

[2]From this point I shall introduce material not only from Colson's book but from time to time from an article I wrote some years ago, "Renewal," *Equipping the Saints* 4, no. 1 (Winter 1990): 8. Used by permission of the publisher.

[3]Charles W. Colson, *Born Again* (Old Tappan, N.J.: Chosen Books, 1976), p. 114 (my emphasis).

[4]Ibid., p. 115.

[5]Ibid., p. 116.

[6]Ibid., p. 117.

[7]Ibid., pp. 116-17. Because Colson is a well-known and highly respected public figure, I have used this particular illustration before, in *Changing on the Inside* (Ann Arbor, Mich.: Servant, 1991) and *Eros Redeemed* (Downers Grove, Ill.: InterVarsity Press, 1993). I want to make it clear that "old-fashioned revival" is still happening.

[8]"Prevenient work" of the Holy Spirit means nothing more than a work of the Holy Spirit prior to conversion, opening our eyes to the truth and thus enabling us to repent.

[9]Colson, *Born Again,* p. 117.

[10]I suggest these two versions because though the NIV translation is perfectly valid, it translates the Greek word *metanoia* to give a New Testament nuance of repentance. This differs from the nuances of words used in the Old Testament. When we combine the two, we begin to understand the process and not just the end result.

[11]He meant that he had been healed spiritually, not physically.

Chapter 5: Repentance: False—& True

[1]Thomas Watson, *The Doctrine of Repentance* (original ed. 1668; reprint Edinburgh: Banner of Truth Trust, 1987), p. 18.

[2]Charles G. Finney, *True and False Repentance* (reprint Grand Rapids, Mich.: Kregel, 1966), p. 12.

[3]Ibid., pp. 13-14.

[4]Charles Colson, *Against the Night* (Ann Arbor, Mich.: Servant, 1989), p. 140.

[5]*The Works of Jonathan Edwards* (reprint Carlisle, Penn.: Banner of Truth Trust, 1984), 7:238.

[6]Ibid., 7:236 (Edwards's capitals).

[7]Ibid., 7:238 (Edwards's emphasis).

[8]Ibid., 7:239.

[9]Charles W. Colson, *Born Again* (Old Tappan, N.J.: Chosen Books, 1976), p. 114.

[10]Jean LaFrance, *Pray to Your Father in Secret* (Sherbrook, Quebec: Editions Pauline, 1987), p. 49.

[11]Ibid.

[12]Finney, *True and False Repentance,* p. 18.

[13]Ibid., p. 15.

[14]Ibid., p. 19.

[15]Ibid.

[16]Ibid., p. 17.

[17]I am fully aware that few Christians nowadays regard masturbation as sinful. If some sins are worse than others, as I believe from Scripture, then sexual sin in general, and masturbation in particular, would be relatively unimportant. Masturbation never used to be talked about. Pastors rarely mention it. But during the last forty years or so, during which time psychology, psychiatry and various forms of Christian counseling have got into the act of giving "expert" opinions on the subject, it has become an understandable and relatively respectable activity, especially for young people. My opinion is at present a minority opinion.

Yet majorities are frequently wrong, and I refuse to follow this one. Masturbation is not merely a habit of young people but continues throughout active sexual life. Some people continue it into their eighties. Significantly many people, in spite of assurances as to its innocence, are deeply ashamed of it, more ashamed than they would be of confessing illicit sexual relationships. Some men, virgins before they married, begin it *after* they have married.

I believe it is sinful because our sexual parts were not designed for masturbation, but for coitus within marriage. We are using our bodies wrongly when we masturbate, and for purposes they were not designed for. While I lament the excessive guilt of past religious condemnation, I regret equally the present permissiveness. Continence would require only an openness between parents and children.

God forgives absolutely. Our problem is coming to him again and again. I deal very much more fully with the topic in *Eros Redeemed* (Downers Grove, Ill.: InterVarsity Press, 1993), chap. 9.

[18]C. S. Lewis, *Mere Christianity,* rev. ed. (New York: Collier Books, 1960), p. 60.

Chapter 6: To Worship a Holy God in Spirit & Truth

[1]Fanny Crosby, "Rescue the Perishing."

[2]Scripture encourages "wine and strong drink" in celebration of God's goodness (Deut 14:22-27) and in his presence, provided that those who throw a feast are generous in their invitations. Scripture encourages alcohol but deplores drunkenness, encourages marriage and calls the marriage bed

undefiled but deplores the wrong use of sex. When we worship sex and alcohol, we really worship the demonic deities behind the altars of sex and alcohol.

[3]Horatius Bonar, "Fill Now My Life."

[4]John Owen, *Sin and Temptation,* abridged ed. (Portland, Ore.: Multnomah Press, 1983), p. 40.

[5]In the eighth century St. Andrew of Crete wrote a hymn that was later translated by John Dykes. My phrase is an allusion to this hymn, "Christian, Do You See Them?" which is found in *Hymns II,* ed. Paul Beckwith, Hughes Huffman and Mark Hunt (Downers Grove, Ill.: InterVarsity Press, 1976), no. 133.

Christian do you feel them,
How they work within,
Striving, tempting, luring,
Goading into sin?

[6]International Fellowship of Evangelical Students, the organization sponsoring the development of InterVarsity-type student fellowships worldwide.

[7]Jacques Ellul, *Money and Power* (Downers Grove, Ill.: InterVarsity Press, 1984), pp. 109-10.

[8]P. T. Forsyth, *God the Holy Father* (Blackwood, South Australia: New Creation, 1987), p. 108.

Chapter 7: Mysterious Wind

[1]I attempt to give a more complete exposition of the purpose of the anointing in the book *When the Spirit Comes With Power* (Downers Grove, Ill.: InterVarsity Press, 1988), pp. 225-40.

[2]For a fuller account of this particular issue, please see ibid., pp. 120-37. I discuss the same question and the current controversy in the appendix of the present book.

[3]Guy Chevreau, *Catch the Fire* (London: Marshall Pickering/Collins, 1994), pp. 17-18.

[4]Leigh Powell, *Chosen by God,* quoted in Tony Sargeant, *The Sacred Anointing* (Wheaton, Ill.: Crossway, 1994), p. 59.

[5]Confusion arises partly because of terminology, but also because of Satan's activity in producing counterfeits of renewal. *Renewal* nowadays seems to mean a powerful move of the Holy Spirit among Christians. The signs and manifestations of such renewals are easily mimicked by insecure people who want a "dose" of the Holy Spirit.

[6]D. Martyn Lloyd-Jones, *Joy Unspeakable: Power and Renewal in the Holy Spirit* (reprint Wheaton, Ill.: Harold Shaw, 1984), pp. 115-16.

[7]I give a much fuller account of the Holy Spirit in *When the Spirit Comes with Power,* dealing with the operations of the Holy Spirit on pp. 229-35.

[8]Lloyd-Jones, *Joy Unspeakable*, p. 21.

[9]Chevreau reports as follows: "The first report was filed in the London *Sunday Telegraph* and the BBC. Shortly thereafter, Toronto television news stations CFTO and CBC featured spots on the 6 o'clock news, followed by articles in the Toronto newspaper *The Globe and Mail, The Hamilton Spectator,* and the international *Time Magazine*" (*Catch the Fire*). Since then New York newspapers, London's *Daily Telegraph* and *Times,* and the *Manchester Guardian* have printed surprisingly favorable reports. My feeling is that we are seeing the early stages of a revival.

[10]From a 1994 sermon preached in Holy Trinity Church, Brompton, London. Eleanor Mumford is the wife of John Mumford, pastor of the Wimbledon Vineyard and leader of the Vineyard movement in Britain.

[11]Lloyd-Jones, *Joy Unspeakable*, p. 141.

[12]Ibid., p. 145.

[13]Ibid., p. 61.

[14]Ibid., pp. 115-16.

[15]John Owen, *Sin and Temptation*, abridged ed. (Portland, Ore.: Multnomah Press, 1983), p. 41.

[16]Ibid., p. 4.

[17]Ibid., p. 5.

[18]Eugene Peterson, *The Message* (Colorado Springs, Colo.: NavPress, 1993), p. 317. Hereafter, quotes from this translation will be labeled "TM" in the text.

[19]Macumba is the name of a powerful Brazilian cult, one of many currently mixing various forms of African witchcraft with Roman Catholic ideas. Another powerful cult is that of the Black Jehovah.

[20]John Bunyan, *The Pilgrim's Progress* (London: Lutterworth, 1947), p. 156.

[21]Owen, *Sin and Temptation*, p. 7.

Chapter 8: Righteousness—Now!

[1]Holiness is a two-phase operation. First God sets you apart for his own exclusive use. This phase is what Paul refers to 1 Corinthians 6:11. The second phase, which continues all our lives, concerns our inner being and our behavior. Once we have been made righteous and set apart, the Holy Spirit begins to deal with the law of sin (our vulnerability to sin). Paul addresses this in detail in Romans 7:14-25.

[2]See chap. 19 of J. I. Packer, *Knowing God*, rev. ed. (Downers Grove, Ill.: InterVarsity Press, 1993), pp. 200-229.

[3]Ibid., p. 228.

[4]John Owen, *Sin and Temptation*, abridged ed. (Portland, Ore.: Multnomah Press, 1983), p. 8.

[5]Quoted in J. C. Ryle, *Holiness* (London: James Clarke, 1956), p. 330, emphasis mine.

[6]James Denney, *The Death of Christ* (New Canaan, Conn.: Keats, 1981), p. 143.

[7]Ibid, p. 178.

[8]R. V. G. Tasker, *The Gospel According to Saint John* (Grand Rapids, Mich.: Eerdmans, 1972), p. 154.

[9]*Calvin's Commentaries* (Grand Rapids, Mich.: Baker Book House, 1993), 18:59.

Chapter 9: Waiting on God

[1]John Greenleaf Whittier, "Dear Lord and Father of Mankind."

[2]John White, *Daring to Draw Near* (Downers Grove, Ill.: InterVarsity Press, 1977).

Chapter 10: The Life of God in the Soul of Man

[1]Henry Scougall, *The Life of God in the Soul of Man* (reprint Harrisonburg, Va.: Sprinkle, 1986), p. 46.

[2]You notice that I make a distinction between church and kingdom. I define *kingdom* as the rule of the King. I wish I could say that he rules in the church, but this would not altogether be true.

[3]The parable of the tares or weeds is found in Matthew 13:24-30, and Christ's own interpretation in verses 36-43. It applies to the kingdom rather than to individual churches, but we must conceive of the real kingdom going on inside the church. In his teaching Jesus warns us to expect that there will be non-Christian members in Christian churches. We are not to ferret them out in an attempt to create a "believers' church"—something that probably never exists. In our search for the false Christians, we would damage the real Christians (13:29). To engage in "witch-hunting" is to try to do what only the angels are supposed to do (13:40-43).

[4]Scougall, *The Life of God*, p. 46.

[5]R. Kearsley, "Perseverance," in *New Dictionary of Theology*, ed. Sinclair B. Ferguson, David F. Wright and J. I. Packer (Downers Grove, Ill.: InterVarsity Press, 1988), pp. 506-7. By the way, John Calvin's *Institutes of Christian Religion* is by no means an inerrant work. It contains statements on some minor matters which I (admittedly a featherweight in matters biblical and theological) cannot agree with. But it represents a magnificent attempt on Calvin's part to limit his thinking to Scripture.

[6]R. T. Jones, "Wrath of God," in *New Dictionary of Theology*, ed. Sinclair B. Ferguson, David F. Wright and J. I. Packer (Downers Grove, Ill.: InterVarsity Press, 1988), p. 732.

[7]Bernard of Clairvaux (born c. 1150), "Jesus, Thou Joy."

[8]J. I. Packer, *Knowing God*, rev. ed. (Downers Grove, Ill.: InterVarsity Press, 1993), p. 118.

[9]Ibid.

[10]Scougall, *The Life of God,* pp. 46-47.

[11]Ibid., p. 47 (italics mine).

[12]I discuss these two subjects more fully in the appendix.

[13]Scougall, *The Life of God,* p. 47.

[14]C. S. Lewis, *Mere Christianity* (New York: Macmillan, 1960), p. 89.

[15]Bernard of Clairvaux, *The Twelve Steps of Humility and Pride* (reprint London: Hodder & Stoughton, 1985), p. 19.

[16]Ibid., p. 20.

[17]John Piper, *The Pleasures of God* (Portland, Ore.: Multnomah Press, 1991), p. 192.

[18]C. S. Lewis, *Mere Christianity* (New York: Collier Books, 1952), p. 114.

Chapter 11: Gazing on Christ

[1]C. S. Lewis, *The Weight of Glory* (reprint New York: Collier/Macmillan, 1980), p. 11.

[2]Charles H. Gabriel, "Glory for Me."

[3]Henry Scougall, *The Life of God in the Soul of Man* (reprint Harrisonburg, Va.: Sprinkle, 1986), p. 63.

[4]Ibid.

[5]John White, *The Iron Sceptre* (Downers Grove, Ill.: InterVarsity Press, 1981).

[6]J. I. Packer, *Knowing God,* rev. ed. (Downers Grove, Ill.: InterVarsity Press, 1993), p. 23.

[7]C. S. Lewis, *The Weight of Glory and Other Essays* (New York: Macmillan, 1980), p. 13.

[8]John Piper, *The Pleasures of God* (Portland, Ore.: Multnomah Presss, 1991), pp. 20-21.

[9]Lewis, *The Weight of Glory,* pp. 11-12.

[10]Ibid., p. 13.

[11]Ibid., p. 16.

Chapter 12: The Passionate People

[1]We, on the other hand, are to bless our enemies, but when occasion demands, to speak the truth plainly. "But I tell you: Love your enemies and pray for those who persecute you . . ." (Mt 5:44).

[2]Eugene Peterson, *The Message* (Colorado Springs, Colo.: NavPress, 1993), p. 389.

[3]Peter Wagner has written about the first, second and third "waves," each a prominent twentieth-century movement by which God has spoken to us about the continuation in his purposes of the power and presence of the Spirit and his gifts.

[4]John Wesley, *The Works of John Wesley,* 3rd ed. (Peabody, Mass.: Hendrickson, 1972), 12:106; see also 1:188.

Chapter 13: Unity & History's End

[1]Eugene Peterson, *The Message* (Colorado Springs, Colo.: NavPress, 1993), p. 389.

[2]Mike Mason, *The Gospel According to Job* (Wheaton, Ill.: Crossway, 1994), p. 50.

[3]Ibid.

[4]*The Works of Jonathan Edwards* (reprint Carlisle, Penn.: Banner of Truth Trust, 1984), 1:539.

[5]Ibid., 1:535.

[6]The quotations are from Iain Murray, *The Puritan Hope* (Edinburgh: Banner of Truth Trust, 1975), pp. xii-xiv.

Appendix: Discerning Truth from Falsity

[1]An account of this conflict can be found in Guy Chevreau, *Catch the Fire* (London: Marshall Pickering/Collins, 1984), pp. 96-98.

[2]Deism is the belief that God wound up the universe like a clock, set it going and then left us to our own devices; that God is not currently present in the universe and does not affect our lives. *Theism*, in contrast, is the belief in an omnipresent God who speaks and acts in the present. Those who deny the miraculous in the present may profess to be theists, but by their manner of life they proclaim that they are really deists.